FATHERS & BABIES

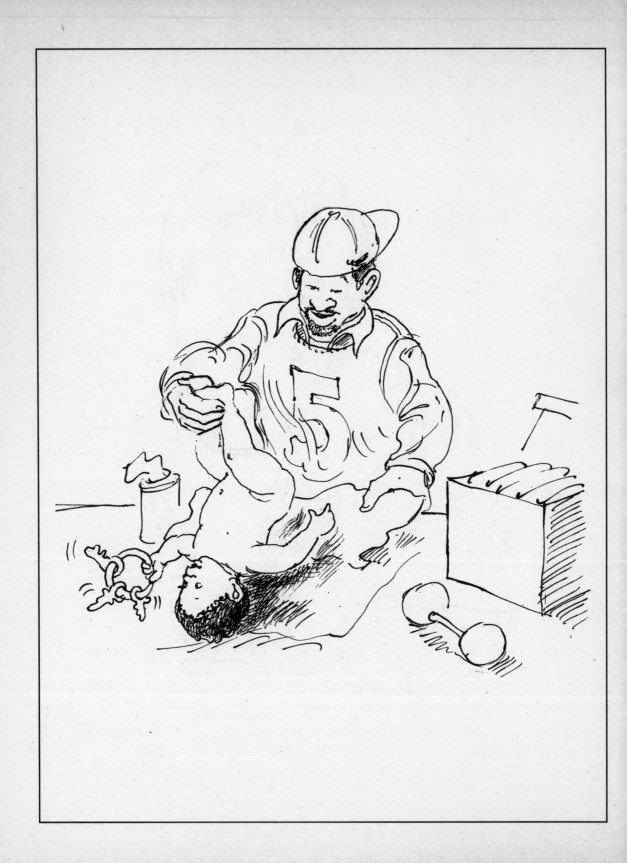

FATHERS & BABIES

How Babies Grow and What They Need from You from Birth to 18 Months

JEAN MARZOLLO
ILLUSTRATED BY IRENE TRIVAS

Quill

A HarperResource Book
An Imprint of HarperCollinsPublishers

HarperCollins books may be purchased for educational, business, or sales promotional use. For information, please write: Special Markets Department, HarperCollins Publishers, Inc., 10 East 53rd Street, New York, NY 10022.

FIRST EDITION

Library of Congress Cataloging-in-Publication Data

Marzollo, Jean.
    Fathers & Babies : how babies grow and what they need from you from birth to 18 months / Jean Marzollo ; illustrated by Irene Trivas.
       p.   cm.
    Includes index.
    ISBN 0-06-096908-3 (pbk.)
    1. Fatherhood.   2. Infants—Care.   3. Father and child.   I. Title.
HQ756.M35   1993
306.874'2—dc20   92-53386

   04 05 06   RRD   30 29 28 27 26

IN MEMORY OF A DEAR FRIEND
AND LOVING FATHER,
DAVID BARCLAY BULLEIT
1944–1992
J.M.

FOR JIM PERRY AND BLAKE TRAENDLY
AND ALL THEIR CHILDREN
I.T.

WITH SPECIAL THANKS TO:

Hugh Van Dusen, Stephanie Gunning, Shelly Perron,
C. Linda Dingler, and Claudyne Bianco at HarperCollins;
our agent Molly Friedrich at Aaron Priest Agency;
Bernard Spodek, professor of early childhood education
at the University of Illinois at Urbana-Champaign; and the following
wonderful parents: Claudio Marzollo, Grace Maccarone, Pam Colangelo
& Jeff Trenner, Carolyn Rossi & Jamie Copeland, Jerome Prince,
Shelley Thornton, Reno Turtur, Michelle & Fabio Fumagalli,
and Roberta Bynes

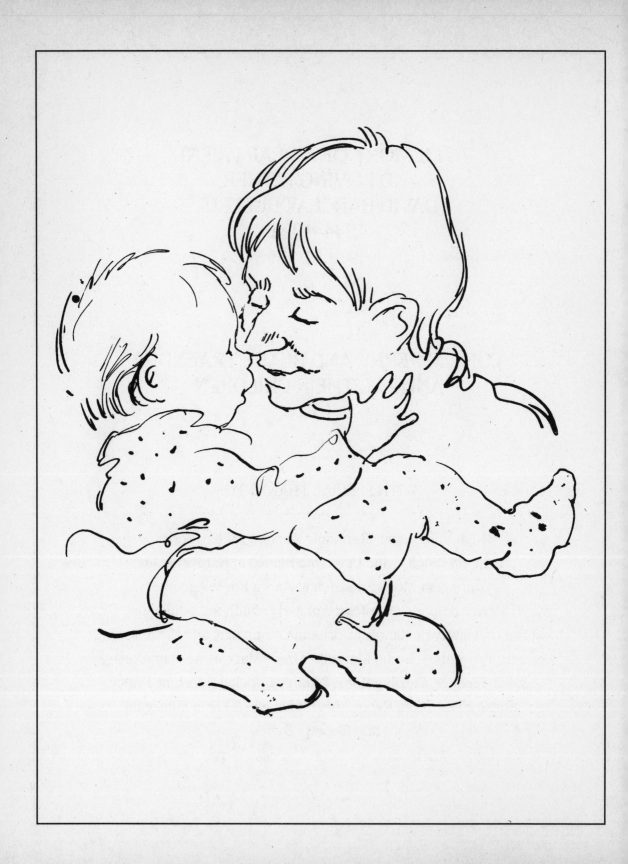

CONTENTS

INTRODUCTION:
FATHERS & BABIES

If you are a new father whose job takes you away from home on workdays, you are at a particular disadvantage when it comes to child care. On the one hand, you are expected by modern society to be an involved father, but, on the other hand, you get very little opportunity to learn the necessary skills. Raising children successfully may be partly a matter of instinct, but mostly it's a matter of effective procedures learned through trial and error.

An old joke for musicians goes like this: A young man asks an older musician, "How do I get to Carnegie Hall?" To which the older man answers, "Practice, my son, practice." You can say the same for fatherhood. It takes practice to know how to handle a crying baby in the middle of the night and to diaper a squiggly baby on a changing table. This very same practice is what makes mothers on maternity leave more relaxed than fathers who have gone back to work and what makes both parents more relaxed with their second child. But first-time fathers who work outside of the home are out of luck when it comes to practice. The world expects them to know how to be dads instantaneously, and this unrealistic expectation causes problems.

Modern miseries.

Consider what happens in many young families in the evening and on weekends. The mother, who may or may not also work away from home (it doesn't matter—either way she needs a break) asks the father to take care of the child. The father is willing, but no matter what he does, the baby cries. The mother gets annoyed because now the baby is howling. Angrily, she takes the baby from the father, who goes back to his newspaper or out for a run, which he hopes will make him feel better, but it doesn't because he feels guilty.

Scenes like this are repeated far too often in the homes of new parents. Working families today are often unhappy simply because they can't figure out how to share child care effectively. No matter how much new parents want their families to function well, they end up quarreling about who does what—with the typical result that the father gets blamed for doing things wrong *and* for not doing enough. Not *caring*, says the wife—and here's where she may be wrong. Because fathers do care. They want to be good fathers who help their children grow up successfully. They just don't know how to go about it.

Fathers need theory and practical advice.

Fathers & Babies will help you become a more practiced and knowledgeable father by giving you simple advice and showing you what to do. (The information in the book is, of course, not just for you; your wife and others who care for your child may find it helpful, too.) The book aims to teach both practical skills *and* child development theory. Developmental theory is useful because it enables you to understand your child and to do the right things at the right time so that your child is nurtured appropriately, neither losing out on important growth experiences nor feeing pushed into them. Most of all, knowledge of child development makes it more fun to play with your baby.

Fathers & Babies will tell you specifically how babies grow and what they need from you from the time they are born until they are one and a half years old. Eighteen incredibly important months—naturally you want to help your child make the most of them, and you want your new family to make the most of them, too—right now. You can never go back and redo these months.

There is a direct correlation between how much fathers help and how happy working mothers are.

If your wife works (and all mothers do, when you think about it), you need to figure out ways to assist at home so that your wife doesn't build up resentment. Learn how to help at night, on weekends, and how to give your wife a night off. The best gift you can give your baby is a happy family, and that is hard to accomplish without a happy mother.

And what about you? Are you happy?

Fatherhood is a new state, easier for some men to adjust to than others. Many fathers (and mothers) feel the loss of freedom acutely. "I couldn't plan spontaneously to go golfing anymore on Saturday morning," said one father. "After working all week, I hated the thought of having to spend all weekend at home taking care of the baby." If you feel similarly trapped, you will feel less so if at least you know what you're doing. Competence is far more enjoyable than ignorance; and ignorance, thank goodness, is curable. It is also not a shameful state. Don't be embarrassed by what you don't know. How could you know it? All that matters is that you now have the impetus to learn and improve.

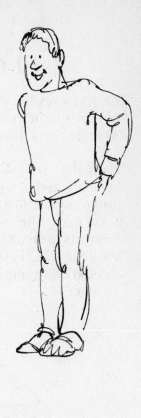

Do yourself and your child a favor.

Don't worry if your child doesn't sit up by seven months, have teeth by eight months, and walk by a year. Time lines are general and meant to indicate a wide range of normal development. If you are concerned about your child's development, talk with your pediatrician. But remember—a rose unfolds by itself without external pressures and training. So it is with a child.

As a parent, you can guide and nurture and, to some extent, shape your child's environment, but you can't control everything, so relax and don't try. Your baby is a marvel, a whole new human being—different, special, unique. No matter how busy you are, take time to enjoy that fact and to receive with grace the gift that has come to you.

CHAPTER ONE:
YOUR NEWBORN BABY

The first week home with a new baby is an amazing experience. As one new father put it, "It's comparable to ocean sailing under full gale conditions." After one particularly harrowing day, this father wrote the following account:

"I've had it. For the last ten days, it seems, I've done much, if not most, of the child care in this house with the notable exception of breast-feeding. My wife's episiotomy became badly infected so she is laid up in bed and requires a good deal of care. She needs her meals brought to her and lots of TLC. Our new son needs his bath, burping, changing, clean laundry, and love. Between the two of them I am going out of my gourd. But how can you get mad at a two-week-old baby and a sick wife?"

Approximate age range: newborn

"The days and nights have become a succession of washing machines, dryers, dishwashers, trips to the A & P, cooking, bringing the baby to my wife for a feeding, feeding my wife, feeding me, getting up, going to bed, and starting all over again. My ulcer is back, so I cook bland food, which is driving my wife crazy. Tonight she burst into tears at the presentation of more white food. I looked down at the tray and started to laugh. She started to laugh too, and for a few moments at least we shared the ridiculous mess of our lives."

Not all fathers have it quite so bad. But even when things go smoothly, you can feel during that first week that a revolution has occurred in your life. The important thing to keep in mind is that the shock of the first week doesn't last. By the time it's over, you'll have begun to master the skills and information on the following pages and started to adapt to changes in your life. It helps to have a relative or friend assist with household chores during the first week or month. But before you invite someone to stay, make sure you and your wife basically like and trust this person. Before you hire a baby nurse, realize that some baby nurses only care for the baby and do not do household chores.

It also helps to keep things as simple as possible during the first week. Don't invite too much company over. And when company comes, don't feel you have to clean up thoroughly or entertain lavishly. Most people understand what you're going through and will be happy just to meet the new baby.

Approximate age range: newborn

ROOTING AND SUCKING

Babies are born with a rooting reflex.

Instinctively babies turn toward the direction of a touch made on one of their cheeks. They will search or "root" for the object that made the touch. If you are trying to feed a baby a bottle, you can put this instinct to work. Just touch the bottle's nipple to the baby's cheek nearest you. A hungry baby will turn toward the nipple with an open mouth.

They are born with a sucking reflex, too.

Babies are born with the ability to suck liquids from a nipple. Some babies can do this instantly while others need a little practice. Babies like to suck, even when they are not hungry, which is why sucking on a pacifier can be soothing to fussy babies. If you use pacifiers, use the safe, orthodontic pacifiers that do not fall apart and that do not distort a baby's mouth.

Approximate age range: newborn

ADVICE FOR FEEDING A NEWBORN

Breast or bottle?

Offer your opinions, and be willing to discuss the matter, but leave the choice up to the mother—and support her choice. If she can't decide, suggest a consultation with your pediatrician. Breast-feeding creates intimacy between the baby and mother as well as passing on the mother's immunities to the baby, but it is a demanding process—and you can't be of much help, though you can feed the baby bottles of expressed breast milk. If and when you and your wife choose to bottle feed exclusively, you can help more.

How to help a nursing mother.

Do whatever you can—make sure your wife has a comfortable rocking chair, run out for breast cream, borrow a breast pump, cook supper, whatever. You can also give your child a bottle of water between feedings to help the baby lengthen the period between feedings and to give yourself a chance to be intimate with your baby, too. You can offer to burp the baby when breast-feeding is over. To do so, put the baby comfortably against your shoulder, and rub or pat the baby's back.

Approximate age range: newborn

INFANT OLYMPICS

Babies are born with amazing skills that they perform reflexively.

Reflex grasping.

Infants can grasp your finger and hold on tight.

Brief head control.

Infants lying facedown on a crib mattress can lift and turn their heads to breathe, a nifty survival skill.

Moro reflex.

Infants react to sudden physical sensations and loud noises by throwing their arms and legs out, almost as if they were pushing the noise away and shouting, "Get out of here!"

Reflex walking.

If you hold your infant with feet touching a surface, your baby will take a few steps. Babies know how to walk, but they can't hold themselves up. It takes about a year for them to get the strength to do that. So if you try this, make sure you support your baby's head and body. Reflexive walking disappears after a few months.

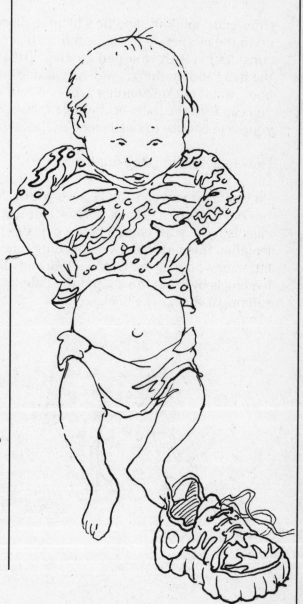

Approximate age range: newborn

TIPS FOR HANDLING INFANTS

Babies' heads wobble on their necks, so hold them in a way that supports both the head and neck. Their backs are weak, so you need to support them there, too. Their skin is sensitive, so handle them gently with warm hands. Babies seem to like it when you lift them up and hold them close to your chest where they can hear your heartbeat. They need, and love, to be cuddled. Wear washable shirts, or put a towel over your shoulder to guard against spit-ups.

Approximate age range: newborn

BABY'S MANY NOISES

Babies are born with various noise-making abilities. They can snort, burp, yawn, sigh, grunt, snore, coo, and cry. They have no sense of manners and will make noises whenever they want. Babies soon learn to make different kinds of cries, from moderate lamentations to full-scale howls. In time, you'll learn to distinguish among your baby's various sounds and know which cries require immediate attention.

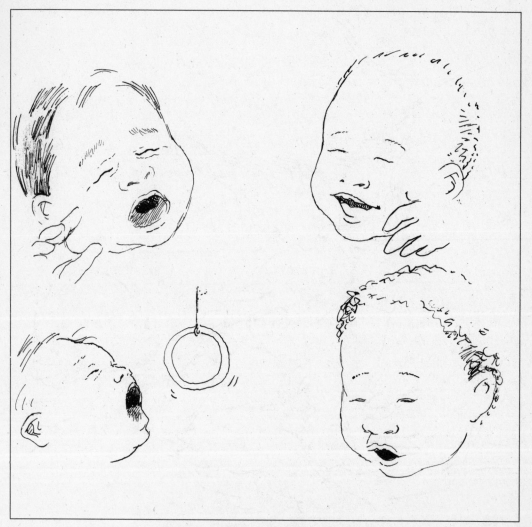

Approximate age range: newborn

How to Soothe a Crying Baby

Newborns cry reflexively when something's bothering them. Their crying usually brings about a reaction from adults. You feed them, change them, hold them, and soothe them. By reacting to your baby's cries with appropriate and caring attention, you not only relieve your baby's physical needs of the moment, but you also begin to teach your baby a sense of trust and two-way communication.

Some things to try when your baby won't stop crying.

• Rocking and singing in a rocking chair.
• Taking a stroll in the baby carriage–indoors or out.
• Going for a ride in the car.
• Laying your baby across your knees and rubbing his/her back.
• Putting your baby over your shoulder with your shoulder pressing into the baby's intestines.
• Walking around with the baby in a front baby carrier.
• Holding Baby very still and whispering a song.
• Winding up the music box mobile hanging over the crib.
• Trying things over again–if Baby rejects the pacifier one minute, he or she may take it the next minute.
• Stepping outside.
• Giving the baby a warm bath.

Observe what your baby likes.

If you jiggle your baby on your shoulder, observe from the reaction if your baby likes this or not. If your baby is overly fussy, bear in mind that some babies have extra sensitive skin. Too much handling and touching causes them discomfort.

When nothing works.

Sometimes it seems that nothing you do can calm your crying baby. After you've fed, burped, changed, rocked, and soothed your baby in every way you know—to no avail, you may have to put your baby down in the crib and let your baby cry it out. Do this especially if your patience has run out. If you react in a negative way (such as with a slap or shaking), you teach your baby not only *not* to trust you, but what's more, your baby only cries harder.

Approximate age range: newborn

LISTENING...

What can infants hear?

They can hear what you hear, but they can't make sense of the sounds.

Loud sounds startle them.

Loud sounds scare newborns and make them throw out their arms and legs in what is called the Moro reflex. (See page 18.)

Babies like soft music.

Perhaps they become used to rhythm in the womb as they hear their mothers' heartbeat and pulse. Outside the womb, babies like soft, steady musical beats.

Babies like to hear people talk and sing to them.

When they are upset, infants like a calming voice, a lullaby—either sung or hummed. When they are bored, they like the funny, high-pitched singsong way people talk to babies.

They also like to hear themselves.

Babies hear their own burps and burbles, and like to experiment with them.

When they sleep, they sleep.

A loud sudden noise may wake a baby, but general background noise doesn't seem to bother most sleeping babies.

Approximate age range: newborn

...And Looking Around

What can babies see?

When babies open their eyes, infants see a world of color, shapes, patterns, and movement. Understandably, they can't take it all in, so it's best to keep their visual world peacefully simple. Infants like to look at things but not for long. Crib decorations aren't interesting to them yet.

They turn to light.

Babies will turn their eyes and heads to light, such as a lamp or window. But if the light is too strong, they will close their eyes.

Not too close and not too far.

Babies are nearsighted; they like to look at things about 8–12" from their faces. If you hold a small doll or teddy bear with a clear face this far away and move it slowly back and forth, some babies will track it briefly with their eyes.

They like human faces.

Of course they do! People's faces have clear features and make interesting noises. Instinctively people hold babies 8–12" away to oogle them. Eye contact, however brief, is important for infants.

Approximate age range: newborn

How to Change a Newborn's Diaper

Gently place your baby on a soft, safe surface. A big, clean, thickly folded towel on the counter next to the sink is fine as long as you block the edge with your body. Infants can fall off, so never leave your baby unattended.

Remove the soiled diaper. Sometimes, you can use clean parts of it to wipe away fecal matter. Clean the baby's bottom. Premoistened baby wipe cloths can be used for this, but they may be too strong for a newborn's skin. It may be better at first to use a baby washcloth, baby soap, and lukewarm water. Holding the baby securely with one hand, use the other to rinse the washcloth. Wash genital folds and crevices carefully. Dry with a soft towel.

You may want to apply a diaper rash ointment, such as zinc oxide or Desitin. Make sure the skin is dry first. Powder is unnecessary, but if you use it, consider cornstarch as an alternative—it's safer if inhaled when sprinkled on. It is unnecessary to use baby lotion or baby oil in addition to an ointment. Apply a clean diaper snugly but not too tightly. If you use cloth diapers, be careful with diaper pins. Set the baby in a safe place while you wash your hands.

Approximate age range: newborn

HOW TO BATHE AN INFANT

The first few baths are scary because wet babies are very slippery. (You can avoid the problem at first by giving your baby sponge baths until the umbilical cord drops off.) For a safe bath, either use a baby bathtub with a built-in infant seat, set your baby in an infant seat right into the sink, or lay your baby on a folded towel in no more than an inch of warm, not hot, water. Always hold your baby very carefully and securely. Use baby soap because it is mild. You probably don't need shampoo yet. Wash your baby gently with a soapy washcloth, then rinse. Keep up a soothing conversation and try to maintain eye contact. Be careful when you lift up your wet baby.

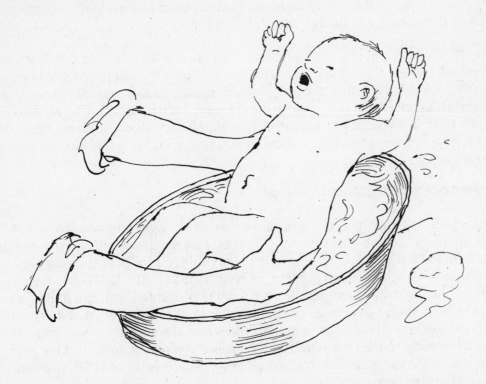

After the bath, set your baby down on a soft towel. Dry and diaper. Although cotton swabs, such as Q-Tips, are a parent's traditional tool for cleaning nostrils and ears, most pediatricians will tell you that used for these purposes, they are a source of danger. If you use them, do so very cautiously. Infants like to be dressed without fuss in soft, comfortable clothes.

Approximate age range: newborn

WAKING AND SLEEPING

Babies in the womb can sleep whenever they want. Once they are born, people want them to switch from womb time to people time. This process takes time. At first babies sleep much of the day and night. Their periods of wakefulness usually come when they are hungry. As they grow day by day and week by week, they take in more food and can go longer between feedings.

Gradually, babies adapt to the rhythms of their homes. After a few weeks they begin to develop a loose schedule of sleeping, eating, and interacting with people. But different babies have different schedules. Some can go four hours between feedings; others only an hour. Parents need to be patient as they get to know the talents and limitations of their babies.

Parents are different, too. At first, some parents are surprised to feel that their sleepy infants are slightly boring. Such parents may not fall head-over-heels in love with their babies until the babies need less sleep and become more interested in observing the world around them. Other parents are crazy about infants right from the start, no matter how much they sleep. It doesn't matter which type of parent you are, as long as you give your baby the warmth and nurture he or she needs.

Helping out with nighttime feedings.

Babies usually wake up at night because they are hungry and need to be fed. Depending on the baby, this means that they may sleep anywhere from one to four hours at a time. Such a schedule is very difficult for parents, who are used to uninterrupted sleep at night. If your baby is bottle fed, you can give some of the nighttime feedings. If your baby is breast-fed, you can find other ways to help. You can change the baby's diaper. You can get up and bring the baby to your wife, if she nurses in bed; and when she's finished, you can return the baby to the crib. Or, in the morning you can fix breakfast for your wife, and in the evening after the last feeding, usually around 11:00, you can put the baby to bed.

How to trim a sleeping baby's nails.

One of the easiest ways to trim a baby's nails is to do so while the baby is sleeping soundly. Hold each finger at the middle knuckle and gently snip.

Approximate age range: newborn

HELPING BABIES SLEEP THROUGH THE NIGHT

The first time that your baby sleeps through a night feeding is an important family milestone because it means that everyone is sleeping longer and better. The first time your baby drops a *second* night feeding is an even bigger step toward getting your family back to normal. It is important to assist the process of getting back to normal and not to impede it. Therefore, make nighttime feedings businesslike. As one pediatrician advises his parents, "Don't even change the baby unless there is a bowel movement." Tend to Baby's essential needs, but do not play with the baby. Do not make nighttime feedings so much fun that your baby wants to hang on to them. The only reason for a nighttime feeding is hunger. If this sounds cold and calculating, remember this: babies need happy families. Happy families need sleep.

Approximate age range: newborn

DEVELOPING TRUST AND THE URGE TO COMMUNICATE

At times newborns will stare at you so intensely that you can almost feel them thinking, "Who and what are you?" The nicer you are to your baby now, the nicer your baby will be—now and forever. That's because by being nice to your baby, you teach your baby to trust in people and the world. You are the world to your baby. What you and others give to your baby, your baby will someday give back to the world. Your baby is born with the urge and potential to communicate. The more communicative you are, the more your child's human potential will be developed.

Approximate age range: newborn

YOUR BABY'S GRANDPARENTS

Grandparents range from infantile to mature, like everybody else. Some are wonderfully helpful after a new baby is born, others less so. If you have the wonderfully helpful type, enjoy them to the fullest. If you have the less-so type, assess the situation realistically in order to make the best of it. If you find that the baby's grandparents are giving too much advice or taking care of the baby in ways that make you or your wife angry, tell them diplomatically. Tactfully suggest other ways they can help—by doing the laundry or preparing meals, for example. Figure out when you and your wife would enjoy a visit and when they might help by baby-sitting. Invite them for those times.

Child care ideas are often different between generations. Listen with respect to grandparents' ideas, but feel free to do things the way you want. It's your baby; you don't have to be defensive. Try to prevent problems from escalating, because grandchild-grandparent relationships can be deeply joyous.

Approximate age range: newborn

CHAPTER TWO:
1 TO 6 MONTHS

One-month-old babies are seasoned with the rich experiences of breathing air, drinking milk, touching cloth, feeling flesh, hearing voices, and, one hopes, feeling very appreciated. Now they can get about the business of reacting to the many new challenges that will come their way. By the time they are six months old, they will have developed many of the skills described on the following pages and, as a result, be increasingly fun to play with.

You too are seasoned—with the rich experiences of holding your baby in your arms, singing lullabies, and realizing what it means to be a father. Slowly, you and your baby are becoming acquainted with each other. By now, your baby probably knows that you like to help out, that you smile a lot, and that you make funny noises. Your baby makes funny noises back, thus beginning what you hope will be many good years of conversation between the two of you. The process starts with the simple but profound desire on both sides to get to know each other.

Approximate age range: 1 to 6 months

Your positive reactions to your baby's behaviors that please you give your lucky baby a sense of being valuable to you—of being able to light up your life. All of this is connected to language development. Throughout your child's life, self-awareness, self-esteem, and the urge to communicate will be inextricably linked.

As a new father you may also be discovering how important it is to develop good communication with your wife. Your relationship has a new angle to it now. You are married to a mother, and she is married to a father. Sometimes these new roles can overwhelm the two of you as you find yourselves only talking about diarrhea and baby food.

It helps to get out and be together again as a couple. If you can't afford a baby-sitter, set up a cooperative arrangement with friends who are in the same predicament. It may be hard to leave your baby with a sitter at first, but that's a normal feeling. Pick a responsible, nurturing person, and leave clear instructions on how to take care of the baby and how to get in touch with you. Tending to your relationship, as well as your baby, may seem overwhelming, but that's life...and the results will be worth it.

Approximate age range: 1 to 6 months

MILK AND FORMULA

In the first four to six months of life babies get their nourishment from breast milk or formula. Both breast milk and formula contain the protein, sugar, and fat that babies need. Your pediatrician may also recommend the use of flouride, vitamins, and/or iron supplements.

Holding your baby.

By now, your baby has become more solid, and you've become more adept at supporting the baby's head and back. You may have experimented with different ways to hold your baby at feeding time. You might like to hold your baby in your arms; you might like to lay your baby in your lap with your baby's head and body comfortably propped on an incline against a crossed leg. Or, you might like to set your baby in an infant seat on a table or couch. The best methods are those in which you and the baby share a closeness and eye contact.

Burping a bigger baby.

By now you generally can predict how much and how often your baby burps—and you may have developed a special technique for burping your baby. You've also, no doubt, discovered how much it helps to put a clean dish towel or cloth diaper over your shoulder to protect your shirt from little spit-ups.

Approximate age range: 1 to 6 months

32

SOLID FOOD

Around the age of four months babies are ready for semisolid foods, such as baby cereal, mashed or strained fruits, yogurt, vegetables, and meats. Some pediatricians advise starting solid foods earlier to help babies go longer between feedings. You can puree baby food yourself or buy it already prepared in baby food jars. Introduce new foods one at a time, waiting several days to make sure your baby isn't allergic to them. Follow the directions on jars and cereal packages for making, warming, and storing baby food. For convenience's sake, note that it's nice but not essential to warm up baby food.

Use a small smooth spoon. Place the spoon in the baby's mouth and withdraw it with an upwards motion, gently scraping off the food on the baby's upper gum. Don't be dismayed if your baby spits food out at first. Either your baby isn't hungry, doesn't like the taste, or hasn't quite mastered the art of gumming and swallowing solid food. Be very patient. Feeding a baby takes longer than you think! And be creative. Mix cereal, yogurt, and applesauce, and try that out. Chat encouragingly with your baby, and sing food songs, if you think that will help. Mealtime is a good time to communicate.

Approximate age range: 1 to 6 months

SAFE CRIBS

Newborns can sleep in small spaces because they are little, used to the womb, and don't move very much. Some parents have their newborns sleep near them for the first month in a bassinet, cradle, or baby carriage. But by the time a baby is a month old, it's time to buy or borrow a crib.

Cribs should conform to the Consumer Product Safety Commission's safety standards, which are as follows: the bars are no farther than 2 3/8" apart, thus preventing babies from getting their heads stuck between the bars; the mattress fits snugly, thus preventing babies from catching their heads between the mattress and the side of the crib; the railing is 26" higher than the lowest level of the mattress support, thus preventing babies from climbing over easily; the hardware is safe and sturdy; all surfaces are smooth; and clear assembly instructions are available for new cribs. A borrowed crib that doesn't meet these standards of safety is wisely rejected.

A crib with only one drop-side is more stable than one with two and costs less. The teething rail should go all around the crib and be secure. Try to pull it off when you test the crib. Also, shake the crib and operate the drop-side. If you buy a crib, it makes sense to buy a standard-size one (30" x 54"), which can be used until your child graduates to a regular bed. Commercial fitted crib sheets are made for standard-size cribs.

Many pediatricians recommend a firm foam mattress—firm so that the baby's head can turn easily, foam in case the baby might be allergic to other stuffings. The mattress should be reversible and have a strong plastic cover with plastic piping at the edges and air vents on the sides.

Crib guards make the bed safer and provide a soft surface for the baby to roll against. They should fit securely and offer no opportunity for your baby's head to get caught under them.

Approximate age range: 1 to 6 months

SLEEPING PROBLEMS & SOLUTIONS

Baby wakes up too much at night.

As babies grow, they give up nighttime feedings. Some babies, however, continue to wake up at night, either because they still have specific biological needs or because they want a little company. If you suspect the latter, try being a little less fun. Take care of business pleasantly, but don't go overboard. Be boring. And be a little suspicious—don't run to every whimper. Babies can learn to put themselves back to sleep when they wake up.

Baby doesn't get enough sleep.

Most three-month-old babies sleep about 15 to 20 hours a day with two or three naps. Most six-month-old babies sleep 14 to 18 hours a day with two or three naps. If your baby needs less sleep, your job as a parent is tougher because you get less relief. But if your pediatrician says your baby is healthy, then you just have to accept reality and try not to be too jealous of your friend whose baby sleeps 12 hours a night and takes two long naps a day.

Baby wants to be rocked but you are too tired.

Try putting crib springs under the crib legs so the crib can be gently rocked by you as you collapse in a nearby chair.

Baby can't sleep at someone else's house.

Buy or borrow a small portable crib that is easily collapsible. Use it as a second crib at home so that your baby gets used to it and therefore will feel at home in it at someone else's house. Variously called crib pens, play cribs, travel cribs, and Port-a-Cribs, these small cribs come in a range of sizes and styles. Some convert to playpens and changing tables. The smaller ones only last until babies can pull themselves up and climb over. The bigger ones last longer but may be harder for you to transport and set up. Try them out before you make a purchase. You can buy fitted sheets for most portable crib mattresses.

Approximate age range: 1 to 6 months

TOILETING

Toileting—as in going to the toilet? Not yet, and not for quite a while. Infants go when they please, so watch out. If you're changing a baby boy, be alert and have a diaper in hand to place over the fountain. Also: be organized. When you take your baby on an outing, bring along a backpack of diapers, wipes, and a plastic bag in which to place used diapers until you can deal with them.

If you treat your baby's bodily functions with care and respect, you'll help your child develop self-esteem and a healthy caring for the human body. Avoid expressing negative reactions to smelly diapers, and try not to use negative adjectives, such as *dirty* and *disgusting* for bowel movements. Change your baby's diapers in a calm, matter-of-fact manner, and, please, don't be one of those men who says that he'll change the diaper if it has #1 in it, but not #2!

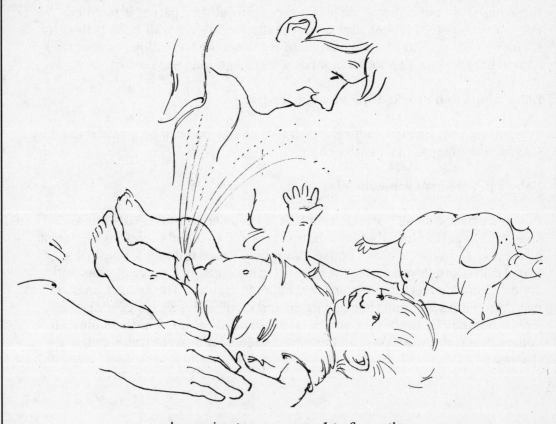

Approximate age range: 1 to 6 months

How to Change a Baby at Someone Else's House

Ask your host to do it for you.

Wrong! Unless, of course, it's your mother, and she *really* wants to do it. Some grandmothers do and will be insulted if you don't let them. Others will be insulted if you take them for granted in this regard. Tricky territory, perhaps, but keep in mind that every host will respect and admire your willingness to go about the business of changing your infant without making a big deal about it.

#1 Find a good spot.

Your host may be able to recommend a place that is safe and out of the flow of traffic. The floor is always a good bet because it's safe and flat. No matter where you are, place a towel or pad underneath.

#2 Have things ready.

You need a fresh diaper, and if your baby has had a bowel movement, you need wipes and a plastic bag handy for the used diaper.

#3 Just do it.

#4 Dispose of the diaper effectively.

Close the plastic bag with a twist tie or a good knot, and ask your host where to put it. Don't throw disposables in a wastepaper basket, where they may not be noticed until they ripen. If you use cloth diapers, store the used ones in a sealed bag until they can be washed.

Approximate age range: 1 to 6 months

BATH TIME FOR A 1-TO-6-MONTH-OLD

One of the nicest and easiest ways to bathe one-to-six-month-olds is to take them into the bathtub with you. Make sure the water is warm, but not hot. First, you should get in the tub and get comfortable. Then, have someone carefully pass the baby to you. Hold the baby's head, neck, and back very securely in your hand or arm and let the baby get used to the water. Babies generally like to float on their backs with you supporting them. The more relaxed you are, the more relaxed your baby will be.

Gently wash the baby with a baby washcloth and mild baby soap. If your baby has a lot of hair, shampoo it with baby shampoo. Work slowly and comfortably. When you are finished washing and you think your baby has had enough time to enjoy the bath, pass your baby very cautiously to someone waiting with a soft dry towel.

Babies also like to be bathed in a baby bathtub and the kitchen sink. Since they usually need, at this age, to be bathed once a day, it makes sense to have bathtime be a special time with its own rituals created by you as you discover what your baby enjoys most—and least.

Approximate age range: 1 to 6 months

DRESSING A 1-TO-6-MONTH-OLD

In one way, babies get less difficult to dress as they grow older. Their limbs become sturdier and easier to guide into the sleeves and legs of garments. Eventually, as babies begin to comprehend what you are doing, they begin to help–pushing that arm right into that sleeve, instantly making your job easier.

On the other hand, as babies grow, they learn to move–and that can be dangerous. You can't leave a baby on a changing table for even a second lest that baby wiggle to the edge and fall off to the floor. Keep fresh diapers, wipes, and clothes handy so that you can reach them from where you are standing. A mobile hung over the changing table gives a baby this age something interesting to look at, but this is not necessary. Your face is every bit as good–in fact, it's really better, especially if you sing, talk, and smile.

Approximate age range: 1 to 6 months

WHAT CAN BABIES SEE NOW?

By the third month.

Babies this age like to stare at nearby objects with interesting shapes. You are one such object. So is a toy you hold in your hand and slowly wave back and forth in front of your baby. So are the colorful objects that hang from crib mobiles.

Babies this age may also discover their hands as fascinating objects to stare at, especially when moving. Discovering that the little hand moving in front of you is your own hand is an amazing discovery for Baby—it's nothing less than the beginning of the discovery of self—and it all comes about from staring...and thinking.

By the fourth month.

Babies begin to exhibit primitive eye-hand coordination. Those hands they've been watching and "owning," if you will—they now realize they can make them move voluntarily.

Babies this age also seem to recognize the people who are taking care of them. Before, they responded to nurturing care, but now, babies seem to look at you and say, "Hey, I've seen you before."

By the fifth month.

If you show your baby part of something familiar, such as part of a favorite toy or part of your face (the rest hidden by a pillow), your baby will seem to recognize the toy or you—and want to see the rest, the whole object. If you hold the toy or your face within reaching distance, your baby will probably reach out to touch the toy or you.

By the sixth month.

Think back several months to when you were holding a much younger baby in your arms. If, back then, you showed your baby your keys and moved them out of sight, your baby wouldn't have cared. If you dropped your keys, you would not have aroused your baby's curiosity. Now show your baby your keys, and your baby will want them. Drop them to the floor, and watch your baby look to see where they fell. Amazing!

Approximate age range: 1 to 6 months

PEOPLE VS. OBJECTS

Objects.

You are wise to learn how to set up situations in which your baby can lie contentedly and look at things—wise for two reasons: (1) your baby learns by looking at things, and (2) while your baby is looking contentedly at things, you can read a few pages in the newspaper. The objects you think your baby would like to look at must be easy for babies to see. While you are reading the paper, you need to feel confident that your baby is in a safe place, such as a crib, playpen, or infant seat that will not tip over. You also need to know that you are not going to be able to read the whole paper because after a while objects loose their appeal. From time to time change the objects that your baby looks at, and change the views your baby sees from his or her infant seat.

People.

After watching objects for a while, your baby may cry out from hunger, fatigue, discomfort, or boredom. If it's boredom, try changing the toys or the view, hoping to re-engage the baby in objects. But realize that your baby is smart enough to know that you win hands down in an Interest Contest with objects. Your baby may want to play with you for a while, and after that, go back to observing objects.

Approximate age range: 1 to 6 months

WHAT CAN BABIES HEAR NOW?

By the fourth month babies will turn toward a voice, as if to find out who's talking. They like to listen to voices and watch the speakers. In the fifth month babies are fascinated by mouths and seem to be connecting the noises you're making with *your* mouth to the noises they can make with *their* mouths. Since listening to sounds and noises is an important part of their lives, it's thoughtful to provide your baby with some good things to listen to: relaxed family members sitting around the table chatting, grandmother's voice telling a story, Auntie singing an Irish tune, a wind chime on the porch, musical mobiles, and so forth. Babies are not always an attentive audience; but if they are neither hungry, tired, nor in discomfort, they probably will be. Remember: babies like to watch the noisemaker making the noise.

AMAZING GRACE....

Approximate age range: 1 to 6 months

MAKING SOUNDS

By the fourth month babies discover that they can produce sounds at will.
Before, they made sounds without necessarily realizing that they were doing
so. Now they not only produce them at will, but if they like the sounds they
make, they also make them again and again and again. Thus, they learn to
amuse themselves at the same time they are educating themselves about their
own talents.

Babies at this age also like to try to imitate simple, and sometimes silly,
sounds you make. This can be a very enjoyable game. Your baby imitates
you, and you imitate your baby. Together the two of you will discover which
sounds you like best to make. As silly as they may seem, such games are an
important part of language development.

Approximate age range: 1 to 6 months

GRASPING THINGS

Babies are born with the reflexive ability to grasp small objects, like your finger. (See *Infant Olympics*, page 18.) This ability is triggered by the sensation of touch on the baby's palm; the baby doesn't really have to think about it. Gradually, however, the grasping reflex fades and is replaced by Baby's conscious discovery of what hands can do. Watching a baby discover hands and learn how to use them voluntarily is fascinating.

At three months, babies look at their hands and seem to wonder what they are. Four-month-old babies can use them to grasp things voluntarily. Five-month-old babies will sit on your lap and grasp objects you give them. Six-month-old babies will play with their hands as if they were wonderful toys.

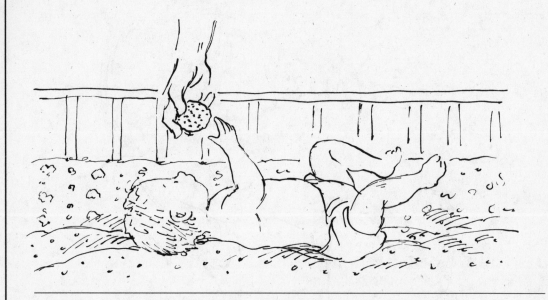

The difference between small muscle skills and large muscle skills.

Skills involving the use of fingers and hands are called "small muscle skills." Children develop them as they play with toys and later as they learn to draw and write. "Large muscle skills" are those that involve larger body parts, such as arms and legs. Large and small muscle skills develop during childhood.

Approximate age range: 1 to 6 months

HOLDING ON TO YOUR KEYS AND THEN LETTING THEM GO

It's one thing to grasp something voluntarily; it's another thing to hold on to it; and it's still another thing to be able to let it go when you want. A two-month-old may only be able to hold on to an object voluntarily for a few seconds while a three-month-old baby may not be able to do much better. But progress is slowly made. A four-month-old baby may be able to grab things with a mittenlike grasp; a five-month-old baby may be able to hold a bottle with one or both hands; and a six-month-old baby may be a proud old pro at reaching, grasping, holding on, and letting go.

Keys as toys.

Why do so many grown-ups take out their keys and hand them to babies? Because key sets are small, make noise, and usually are available, wherever you are. If you hand your baby your keys and your baby grasps them and drops them, don't put your keys away. Pick up your keys and try again. Try to figure out what stage your baby is at, and invent a little game on that level. It may be that your baby just wants to watch you jingle your keys. Or to bat at them. Or to hold them and drop them. To you, jiggling keys or picking them up repeatedly from the floor may be boring, but if your baby genuinely likes the game, you can feel confident that your baby is getting something out of it.

Two key cautions.

(1) Probably your baby is not yet able to bring hand to mouth, but if he or she is, watch out. Most likely your keys are not clean enough to be mouthed.

(2) Young babies can't let go voluntarily. Your baby may be sick of shaking your keys and want you to take them away.

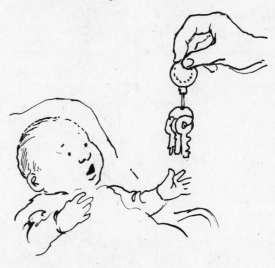

Approximate age range: 1 to 6 months

Eye-Hand Coordination

As babies' eyes develop and they discover their hands, they put the two together in a process of eye-hand coordination that will continue into adulthood. As a parent, you don't really have to teach eye-hand coordination; babies will teach it to themselves. All you have to do is give them opportunities to practice these skills. You do this by playing with them, giving them things to hold, and being patient as they are learning. You also help by respecting your baby's mission.

By being aware of your baby's actions, you catch some marvelous moments. For example, you might look over and see your baby holding something in one hand and waving the other hand in the air. You notice that your baby is looking from the object to the other hand, and very possibly wondering in a wordless way, "What are the possibilities here?" All of a sudden, your baby passes the object to the other hand. Eureka! This is very exciting. But *you* don't need to do anything—your baby is learning on his or her own. Still, you wonder. Will your baby do it again? Maybe, maybe not; if not, maybe tomorrow or the next day and then...with practice...almost every time.

Approximate age range: 1 to 6 months

INTELLIGENCE DEVELOPS

Intelligence develops rapidly in babies as they develop a sense of self and their ability to do things. They notice that what they do causes reactions. Without words they experience themselves as subjects, their actions as verbs, and the things they affect as objects. *I can shake my rattle and make noise. I can pat your face. I can hit my cradle gym.* By the fifth month babies exhibit a sense of cause and effect.

What can you do to help intelligence develop?

Provide small, safe objects and toys, such as rattles (see pages 50–51), for your baby to manipulate. Provide an interesting environment to look at, touch, and listen to. Play games with your baby that are neither too hard nor too easy—but just right for *your* baby. Be responsive. Communicate.

Approximate age range: 1 to 6 months

REACHING FOR THINGS

Babies are so valiant! No matter how clumsy they are, they don't give up. They reach for things and miss, reach and miss. Again and again. They have a wonderful inner drive that keeps them going, and their persistence usually pays off. Slowly but steadily over the first six months of life, they develop more and more skills.

Reaching for things is a perfect example of this process. A three-month-old baby may reach unsuccessfully with two closed fists for the rattle you hold out. Three months later, the same child may reach with one hand and easily grasp the rattle. Your job in the process is to hold out safe things for your baby to try to reach, be sympathetic and optimistic when your baby fails, and share the job when your baby succeeds.

Watch out!

Watch out for unsafe things that your baby wants to reach for. Put away breakables that can get knocked over by babies innocently trying out their new skills. And watch out for hot, sharp, and otherwise dangerous things that Baby may unsuspectingly want to reach out and touch.

Approximate age range: 1 to 6 months

BATTING AT THINGS

Batting at things is different from reaching and trying to grab them. Here, the object is just to smack something and watch it move in reaction. Babies may start doing this as early as two months, but at first they are not very good at hitting the target. By four months they are much better.

Babies like to bat at toys and mobiles; they also like to bat at people, especially at people's faces. Young siblings can get upset at this and understandably may want to hit back. Explain to young children that babies don't want to hurt them—they are just trying to learn how to hit targets. Help children learn how to play batting games with babies by holding up a stuffed animal for the baby to bat. Explain that the reason babies bat at faces is that faces are so interesting to babies.

Approximate age range: 1 to 6 months

RATTLE PLAY

Rattles are the perfect toy for babies who are learning to reach, grab, and bat. Because rattles make noise, babies experience the results of their actions not only visually but also auditorily. Here are some rattle games to play with your baby; you'll, no doubt, invent more.

Game #1:
Can you reach it?

Hold a rattle out in front of your baby for him or her to try to reach.

Game #2:
Can you hold on to it?

See if your baby can hold the rattle. If the rattle is too big and heavy, try a lighter one. If your baby can't hold the rattle, make a game of catching the rattle as it drops.

Game #3:
Can you let it go?

As babies grow, they learn to let go of things. Letting go is an action that can be the basis of many games, such as: *I give it to you, and then you give it to me! (Repeat)*

Game #4:
Can you bat it?

Hold the rattle loosely in your hand so that when your baby strikes at it, it drops.

Approximate age range: 1 to 6 months

DIFFERENT KINDS OF RATTLES

Different rattles are fascinating to babies in different ways. Plastic safety pin rattles are lightweight and easy to hold. So are plastic keys or disks on a chain.

See-through rattles enable babies to see what's rattling around inside, thereby helping babies pursue their studies of cause and effect.

Wooden rattles have a nice solid feel but may be too heavy at first.

Rattle safety checklist.

• Rattles should not be so small that babies can put the whole thing in their mouths, possibly inhibiting breathing.

• Rattles for younger babies should be lightweight so that babies can hold and shake them easily.

• Rattles should be made of non-toxic materials and painted with non-toxic paint.

• Rattles should be solidly built. Inspect each rattle for parts that can be removed and possibly swallowed.

• Rattles and other toys should be clean enough to go in Baby's mouth. When needed, give rattles and other toys a wash.

Approximate age range: 1 to 6 months

KICKING AT THINGS

Cradle gyms and mobiles.

Babies like to lie on their backs and kick in the air at interesting things above them. But you don't have to hold things in the air because toy and baby equipment manufacturers make interesting cradle gyms and mobiles that are perfect for babies who want to kick up their heels. You can also make them yourself.

How to make a rattle mobile.

Tie safe rattles securely on sturdy strings that hang from a bar over the baby's crib or playpen. Your baby should be able to make noise by kicking or batting at the rattles. Make sure your baby cannot get caught in the strings. If you're unsure of the safety of the mobile you devise, remove it and put it away when you're not watching the baby.

Approximate age range: 1 to 6 months

Is There Such a Thing as Too Much Praise?

At a certain point, your baby will discover that he or she can make a rattle mobile or cradle gym move and make noise by kicking it. The movement and noise are very rewarding to Baby because Baby produced it. Such an outcome is really all the positive reinforcement Baby needs. You therefore don't need to praise your baby madly for every stunning accomplishment. Or, to put it another way, your baby doesn't always need your praise. Sometimes it's wise to let children experience their accomplishments privately so that they know they are learning for themselves, not for you. Too much praise over the years can teach them otherwise. But let there be no misunderstanding here—your praise is very important to your child. It's just that there are times when it isn't really necessary.

Approximate age range: 1 to 6 months

OOCHING AROUND

Precrawling babies somehow manage to ooch around in their cribs. You set them down in the middle of the crib and find them later over in the corner. Make sure your crib is safe (see page 34) and that bumper pads are held down securely so that your baby can't get caught underneath them.

Approximate age range: 1 to 6 months

ATTEMPTS AT CRAWLING

As babies grow, they get better at ooching and scooching. They wiggle and swim around in ways that anticipate later crawling. This activity is good for babies, so put your baby down in a clean, soft place on the floor from time to time for this kind of exercise. A clean baby blanket on a rug is fine. Keep your eye on the baby to make sure he or she doesn't get tangled up in the blanket.

"I can't believe how interesting it is to watch my little girl trying to crawl," says a new father. "She works so hard, I figure if she works that hard now, just imagine what she'll do when she's fifteen. Maybe she'll be on the track team!"

Approximate age range: 1 to 6 months

THE SECURITY OF ROUTINES

Babies like routines. They like knowing what to expect when you start to feed them or change them. Routines help them anticipate what will happen next. Since older children and grown-ups like routines too, it's worth it to take a little time and figure out which routines make your family function smoothly.

Family routines.

New babies change family routines. For a while, life at home seems chaotic, but gradually you create routines that work, and you settle into them. Make sure the new routines work for everyone, though, and that no one has taken on an unfair share of work and responsibility.

Encourage family democracy. When things don't work out, sit down and discuss what's wrong. At these meetings look together at ideas for better solutions, agree to try out new arrangments, and identify improvements that are already working in your family so that you can make them part of your routines.

Keeping channels of communication open between you and everyone else caring for your child is key to solving problems as they arise and not letting them fester.

Your own special routines with Baby.

Everyone who cares for Baby doesn't have to do it the same way. Feel free to create your own procedures for feeding, bathing, and changing your baby. Find out what works best for you and the baby, and repeat your methods. You might, for example, say the same thing every time you greet your baby in the morning or sing the same song every night at bedtime.

GOOD MORNING MR. PRESIDENT!

Approximate age range: 1 to 6 months

GAMES PARENTS PLAY

While expressing their love for their children, parents often exhibit the nasty but very human side effect of parental competitiveness. In order to promote their own children's worth to the world at large, parents compare ad nauseam their children's abilities with other children's abilities. Lest you find yourself indulging in this parental vice, learn to identify the most common competitive games parents play so that you can stop yourself from indulging:

Game #1:
Most brilliant child.

The most brilliant child says "Da-Da" before all other babies at the park, etc.

Game #2:
Most coordinated child.

The most coordinated child rolls over before all other babies at the park, etc.

Game #3:
Most mature child.

The most mature child sleeps through the night at two weeks, never wants to suck on a pacifier, and gets the first teeth, etc.

Game #4:
Best parents.

The best parents spend the most time with their children, have the best toys and baby equipment, and feed their children the healthiest food, etc.

RULES FOR BRAGGING

1. Parents and baby-sitters can brag a little.
2. Grandparents can brag as much as they want—but they also should avoid making invidious comparisons with other children.

Approximate age range: 1 to 6 months

EASIER TO HOLD

The more babies grow, the easier they are to hold. Their back muscles and neck muscles become stronger so that babies can support themselves more. You'll find it easier now to take them around with you. But bear in mind that their heads are still top heavy. Be alert to sudden motions that may make it necessary for you to support your baby's head and neck.

Approximate age range: 1 to 6 months

BABY PUSH-UPS

As babies develop stronger back and neck muscles, they naturally want to use them. To this end, they try to do their own version of push-ups on the changing table and in their cribs. This is great exercise! Babies seem to set and follow their own program. By the time they're nine to twelve months old, they'll be able to lift their heads up longer and longer, lift their chests off the ground, and even lift up their whole bodies into crawling position. For now, appreciate your baby's push-ups for what they are—a start. To help your baby get this form of exercise, put your baby down often on his or her stomach.

Approximate age range: 1 to 6 months

LYING ON BACK, TRIES TO ROLL OVER

At some point when they are ready, usually between the fourth and sixth month, babies try to roll over. This is a good activity to encourage because it develops arm and chest muscles that babies will need later in order to sit up. You may notice that, when placed stomach down, babies will roll from side to side—an excellent exercise. In time, this motion will develop into a full roll-over, and babies will end up on their backs. Usually babies learn how to roll over from front to back before they learn how to roll from back to front.

Approximate age range: 1 to 6 months

ROLLOVER GAMES

Sideways roll.

Place your baby stomach down on your changing table or mattress. Then gently roll your baby over gently onto his or her side. See what happens. If your baby rolls back to the stomach, that's okay. If your baby rolls to the back, that's good, too. Make whatever happens be fun. If your baby likes the activity, continue. If not, discontinue.

Follow the toy.

Place your baby stomach down and hold a toy in front of him or her. Move it back and forth slowly in her field of vision. Then move the toy over one of your baby's shoulder so that your baby has to turn to see it. Keep moving the toy toward your baby's back. Your baby may roll over in order to keep watching it. While you're playing these games, talk about them and cheer your baby on.

Approximate age range: 1 to 6 months

THUMB SUCKING

Babies may enjoy sucking their thumbs and fingers. You might want to try to have them suck a pacifier instead, but don't get upset if your plan doesn't work. It's not really worth it because babies don't have the kind of self-control required to stop thumb sucking. In time, your baby will become interested in other objects to hold and to mouth. If thumb sucking continues past age two, consult your pediatrician for modern, effective, and humane methods to help children gradually drop the habit.

Approximate age range: 1 to 6 months

EARLY TEETHING

By six months some babies may have two lower front teeth. Signs of teething are drooling, crying, being fussy, having a runny nose, running a fever, mouthing things, and sucking fingers and the thumb.

What you can do.

• Keep a bib on the baby to catch and wipe drool.

• Provide your baby with teething toys.

• Try putting teething toys in the refrigerator so that they will be cold against Baby's sore gums.

• Consult your pediatrician if your baby seems to be in great pain. Medication may relieve suffering.

• Be a little extra patient with your baby's fussiness.

• At the same time, don't overdo your ministrations during the night. In spite of teething, you want your baby to make or sustain progress toward the goal of sleeping through the night.

Approximate age range: 1 to 6 months

FIRST SMILE

Babies usually smile when they are about three months old. Everyone who helps to take care of Baby gets to see a "first" smile. So, if you are away on a business trip and your wife tells you the baby has smiled for the first time, be thrilled for her. Don't feel that you missed out. You'll get your first smile when you return home.

Approximate age range: 1 to 6 months

A Father's Reaction to His Baby's First Smile

"When Charlie smiled at me for the first time, I burst into tears," admits a fifty-five-year-old first-time father. "I was overwhelmed by the beauty of it all. No new car or pair of skis has ever come close to making me so happy. All those sleepless nights and the endless colic weren't important anymore."

Approximate age range: 1 to 6 months

AH-GOO:
THE BEGINNINGS OF SPEECH

Very young babies have the ability to make sounds; and, as they grow, they do so with increasing variety. They laugh, gurgle, coo and goo, squeak, and squeal, enjoying their own spectacular performances.

Parents enjoy them, too, and usually, no matter how silly they sound, they copy their babies willingly. For example, if your baby has been saying, "Ah-goo," chances are you have been saying, "Ah-goo," too—over and over again.

Beause of your enthusiastic and responsive reaction, your baby has been learning something wonderful—that sounds can have meaning. At first the meaning may just be that Baby's sounds cause you to make sounds, too. Later, sounds will turn into language.

Your babbling baby will now start to develop a repertoire of sounds that constitute beginning speech. Your baby's urge is always to improve, so don't worry about baby talk. If Baby calls his bottle a "ba-ba," you can call it a "ba-ba," too, although as time goes on, it's helpful to reflect Baby's language with correct forms, such as, in this case, by saying "bottle."

For some parents, the true joys of parenthood don't start until they communicate with their babies. As one parent said, "At first it was hard to communicate with the baby. There was dead silence when I changed or fed her, and I felt like an idiot babbling away. Now my baby coos, smiles and looks at everything with big eyes, and I adore holding her and cooing back."

Approximate age range: 1 to 6 months

Awareness of Self

Every time your baby makes a noise or performs an action that brings about a response from people or the baby's environment, self-awareness grows. When your baby shakes a rattle and makes a sound that he or she can hear, self-awareness grows. When your baby moves in front of a mirror and sees the same movement reflected in the mirror, self-awareness grows.

Awareness of Others

Around the third month babies may seem to recognize you, and this recognition will probably give you a new burst of pride in fatherhood. Interestingly, babies this age and younger don't seem to react one way or the other to strangers, so if you hire a new baby-sitter, your baby probably won't react. Around the fifth month, however, babies seem to recognize strangers as such. If you hire a baby-sitter now, you may have to be more sensitive to your baby's reaction.

Approximate age range: 1 to 6 months

DIFFERENT KINDS OF CRIES

As they grow, babies learn to make different kinds of cries. You, in turn, learn to distinguish between these cries and to react accordingly.

Cry of hunger.

This persistent cry usually comes around Baby's dinnertime. The best way to deal with it is to give Baby something to eat. If the meal isn't ready, a bottle of water or a teething biscuit may stave off hunger.

Cry of illness or pain.

This cry is loud and persistent if something just hurt your baby, or moderately loud and persistent if the pain or illness is lasting. *Don't hesitate to call the pediatrician if your instincts tell you to.*

Cry of shock and possible pain.

Sometimes your baby has bumped into something and is more shocked than hurt. A little TLC goes a long way. Don't overreact.

Fussy, teething cry.

This cry of frustration is accompanied by drooling and the mouthing of things. You may be able to see emerging teeth. Feel sorry for your baby. Painful gums are no fun. See page 99 for ideas on how to help.

Midnight can't-sleep cry.

This cry is the most dreaded one parents have to face. Sometimes it means Baby is hungry or in discomfort and genuinely needs help. Sometimes, however, it's actually a cry of exhaustion, but Baby is too worked up to sleep. Usually the crying releases the tension and winds down at long last into sleep.

Manipulative whine.

Babies are not born with this. They develop it when they learn what kind of a reaction their cries bring. You'll be able to recognize this cry by its phoney ring. The best thing to do is check out the possible reasons for the cry. If you find none and suspect the cry is phoney, then ignore it.

Approximate age range: 1 to 6 months

DISCIPLINE

The key to keeping babies on an even keel is to be consistent in your actions with them and to prevent unnecessary stress in their lives. For example, hunger, fatigue, and overstimulation make babies upset, but usually you can prevent these things from happening.

Sometimes it *seems* that babies cry for no good reason other than to annoy you. This isn't really true, but you feel annoyed anyway. When you're annoyed and your baby's upset, it's hard to calm things down. Try rocking your baby, taking your baby for a walk, putting your baby in the stroller and strolling to and fro in your home. Sometimes all that's needed is a repetitive, gentle motion.

Don't spank your baby.

If you feel your temper starting to snap, put your baby in the crib and go out of the room to calm down. Don't hit your baby, thinking that spanking will provide the discipline your "misbehaving" baby needs. Spanking will only make both of you feel worse. Turn on some music, and discipline yourself to stay cool. Don't feel guilty. Most parents get in a rage at one time or another. Remember: *feeling* like hitting your child is okay; *doing it* isn't.

Saying "no."

Babies can't help it. They make messes. They mess food on their faces, and sometimes they make messes with the contents of their diapers. They don't know better yet. But they want to learn and are eager to please you, so you can slowly begin to say "no" gently but firmly to actions you do not want them to do. Your "no" has meaning if: (1) you mean it, (2) are consistent, (3) don't overuse the word, and (4) usually express satisfaction with your child.

Approximate age range: 1 to 6 months

LISTENING TO YOU

Whenever you feel comfortable doing so, talk as you are taking care of your baby. Your baby will enjoy listening to you. And let your baby see your face as you talk, watch your lips move and your eyes twinkle. You don't have to talk in that funny high-pitched way that grown-ups often talk to babies, though you can if you want to. You also can use your normal tone of voice and talk about what's on your mind: the weather, the stock reports, the baseball scores. Your baby may turn out to be the best listener in your life.

Approximate age range: 1 to 6 months

Sounds & Music

At times, amuse your baby by making odd sounds with your voice, alternating high and low tones, fast and slow rhythms, loud and soft sounds. Whispering is a fascinating sound affect. If you're chanting nursery rhymes, try whispering a verse and then saying one in your normal voice.

By all means, sing to your growing baby. Sing or hum songs you learned when you were a child or your favorite songs from any era. Don't be shy. Babies have no idea if you are singing off or on key, or if you are making up the words.

Make music and interesting sounds a part of your baby's immediate world. Hang wind chimes in the window. Play a music box at the beginning of Baby's nap. But avoid overstimulating your baby with too much noise and music. Remember that peace and quiet are nice, too, for people of all ages, including little babies.

BABY LOVE, BABY LOVE I NEED YOU...

Approximate age range: 1 to 6 months

DON'T RUSH SITTING

Young babies at three months have soft spines and therefore cannot sit up. They should either be placed in a lying down position or held in a reclining position. Infant seats are made with the correct slant.

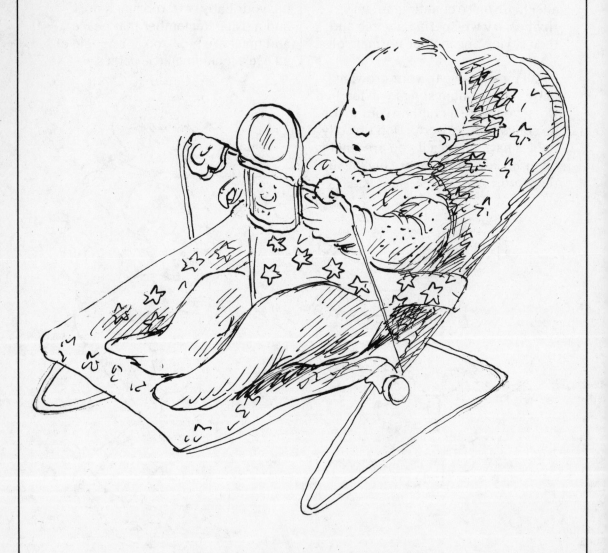

Approximate age range: 1 to 6 months

SITTING WITH HELP

Between five and seven months your baby may enjoy sitting in your lap with your solid support behind him or her. In time your baby will need your support less and less. Take your cues from your baby. When your baby is ready to practice sitting, he or she will let you know. As your baby progresses at sitting, you can set him or her down on the rug with pillows propped around for stability and safety. Stay close by to help if baby falls over and can't sit up again.

Approximate age range: 1 to 6 months

STANDS WITH HELP
FOR A BRIEF TIME

Infants move their legs in a reflexive walking motion when held up (see page 18), but this reflex fades after a month or two. Let it go. Don't try to build on this reflex and push babies to learn to walk. They'll walk when they're ready as part of a normal sequence of development. Around six months babies like to be held up to stand. They like to push against the floor or your legs in a kind of leg-strengthening exercise they develop on their own. They'll do this as long as necessary; you don't have to try to get them to practice it, or urge them to practice more. Babies know best what to do; all you need to do is respond.

Approximate age range: 1 to 6 months

WHEN TO USE WHAT

Frontpacks and backpacks.

Front baby carriers that hold babies snugly to your chest much as you hold a baby in your arms are great because they support the baby's back. Not until babies can sit up by themselves (around seven months, usually) are they ready for backpacks.

LOOKING GOOD..

High chairs.

Until their backs strengthen enough to sit up, babies slump too much to be comfortable and safe in high chairs.

Baby swings.

Baby swings are okay if they hold babies in a tilted or horizontal position. They're not okay if young babies with weak backs are made to sit up in the seat.

Walkers.

Babies aren't ready for walkers until they can sit up well. Even then, some people feel walkers are developmentally inappropriate. (See page 173.)

Jumpers.

Jumpers enable babies to jump up and down before their backs are strong, and some babies do love this activity. But jumpers are controversial. Some people feel they can be harmful to babies' joints and bones. Jumpers can also be unsafe, so watch your baby the whole time he or she is in a jumper. Jumpers, like walkers, can be considered developmentally inappropriate.

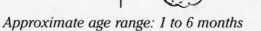

Approximate age range: 1 to 6 months

THE EASY PART OF BEING A FATHER

Giving love.

Being loved.

Being trusted.

Feeling strong.

Feeling important.

Feeling valuable.

Having an heir.

THE HARD PART
OF BEING A FATHER

The endless schlepping.

The constant demands.

The loss of freedom.

The lack of sleep.

The expenses.

The fears.

Less sex.

CHAPTER THREE:
6 TO 9 MONTHS

Six-to-nine-month-old babies are amazing. First of all, they use their hands to do more and more different kinds of things. If you know what these things are, you'll be able to appreciate your child's progress and help it along in playful ways. Babies this age also use their legs to kick at crib gyms and their arms to hold on to you when you pick them up.

When their backs become strong enough, babies sit up, an important milestone. It makes sense that babies who are sitting and holding things will want to talk about them, and they begin to do so in an intriguing language they invent called babbling. Sitting, holding, babbling—astonishing accomplishments for you to witness and enjoy during these exciting months; you will enjoy them the most if you know what's going on.

Approximate age range: 6 to 9 months

As you take care of your baby, remember to take care of everyone else in your family, too, including your wife and yourself. A big responsibility? Yes. Sometimes feels like too much of a burden? Yes. Identifying problems as they occur will lessen the buildup of tensions. Communication is essential. You don't have to know all the answers, but if you discuss difficulties openly, honestly, and sensitively with your wife, baby-sitter, and other children in the family, you'll be far closer to solutions than if you clam up and let resentments smolder. Don't grieve over past mistakes; acknowledge them and move on.

Tend to your relationship. Don't just work out problems that inevitably occur, but try also to create positive experiences when the two of you can be together. After the baby's in bed, watch TV together, snuggling on the couch. On rainy Saturdays, take advantage of the baby's nap to take one together yourselves. If sex occurs, fine; but don't make that the goal. And don't convey the idea that you'll not be happy unless the two of you make love. There are so many things that parents *have* to do. Making love shouldn't be one of them. Also: don't sabotage yourself by making sexual advances at times when sex is impossible. Be a little more strategic...and considerate, both to yourself and to your wife. Creativity, sensitivity, and patience will pay off because the best gift you can give your child is a happy family, and a satisfying sex life for parents is a justifiably important component of a happy family life.

Approximate age range: 6 to 9 months

HOLDING THE BOTTLE

Babies used to drinking liquids from a bottle have watched you hold their bottle in your hands. Eventually, being smart little tykes, they will reach out for the bottle themselves. When this happens, be gracious. Let your baby try holding the bottle with you. At first babies need help, but someday they will be able to support the bottle with their own two hands. They also will be able to take it from you and hoist it to their mouths.

Babies who can hold their bottles themselves have reached a milestone. This milestone can leave you regretting the end of the close connection experienced when you feed your baby a bottle. On the other hand, your baby's ability to hold the bottle makes your life easier and your baby's life more satisfying, since he or she can now experience more self-control.

Tip: the lighter the bottles, the easier they are for babies to hold. Some bottles have straws in them, enabling babies to hold them upright and still suck them. Babies rarely suck air with such bottles. However, you may feel the advantages of these bottles is offset by the necessity of cleaning more bottle parts.

Approximate age range: 6 to 9 months

WEANING

Breast-feeding mothers wean their babies from breast to bottle or cup at different times. The decision usually hinges on how much the mothers enjoy breast-feeding, how important they think it is for the baby, and how conveniently breast-feeding fits into their daily schedule. There is no right or wrong choice to make; it is a personal decision.

Regardless of timing, the process of weaning affects mothers differently. Some mothers hate to give up breast-feeding, others can't wait, and many feel mixed. They miss the intimacy but like their newfound freedom. Be sensitive to your wife's feelings about the matter and accept them for what they are. Realize that once your wife weans your baby, you can help with more feedings.

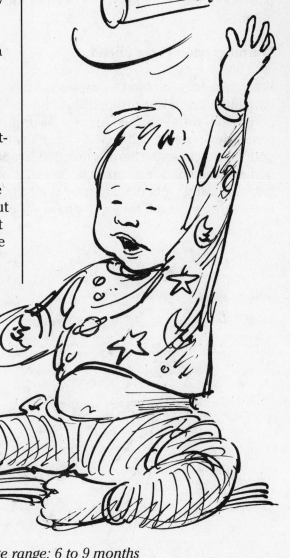

Approximate age range: 6 to 9 months

EATING SOLID FOODS

Usually, babies are eating some solid food by this time (see page 33). It makes a certain amount of common sense that, since they are sprouting teeth during this period, they should have a little something to chomp around on. By this age, too, they can sit up to eat—with or without your support—and sitting up helps the food go down. Once babies are used to swallowing smooth, strained baby food, they can be given chunkier food to eat, usually around seven months.

Warning: parent trap ahead.

When to feed solid food to babies is one of those issues that parents often feel emotional, and even competitive, about. If your wife is breast-feeding happily and wants, with your pediatrician's support, to continue the baby on a diet primarily of breast milk *and* if your baby is gaining weight normally, support your wife's choice. There is no need to add more solid foods if your wife and pediatrician don't want to. The fact that other babies the same age as your baby are eating lots of solid food doesn't really matter. What matters is that babies thrive, which they can do on various healthy diets.

Approximate age range: 6 to 9 months

QUICK & EASY BABY FOOD RECIPES

Cereal treat.
Mix baby cereal with cottage cheese.

Baby's best dessert.
Mix baby food fruit with yogurt.

Meal-in-one.
Mix baby food fruit, baby cereal, and yogurt or cottage cheese.

Most portable snack.
A soft banana: mash it or slice it.

Pureed chicken.
Boil, skin, bone, chop, and blend chicken. Moisten with chicken broth.

Vegetable puree.
Cook vegetables. Blend with chicken broth or some of their cooking water.

Leftovers.
Blend yesterday's leftovers of chicken or meat with broth, milk, or yogurt.

Frozen food.
Puree cooked meats and/or vegetables in large batches. Freeze in ice cube trays. When frozen, remove cubes and store in plastic bags in the freezer.

Blender soup.

Put a high quality brand of canned soup in the blender to make an easy pureed mush. This works well when you're visiting in other people's homes.

Easiest of all.
Use commercial baby food. Check the labels for additives, such as salt, sugar, and MSG, which used to be common, but now are not.

Finger food.
When your baby can sit up in the high chair, try some finger foods. Babies love them! (See page 140.)

Approximate age range: 6 to 9 months

SLEEPING PROBLEMS

Waking up at night.

Most babies between the ages of six and nine months sleep pretty well at night and get about 14 to 18 hours of sleep in a day. After your child has established the ability to sleep through the night, though, you may be surprised one night to hear that old familiar cry. It's probably a teething cry, not a hunger cry, so, whatever you do, don't feed the baby. If you do, you may start your child on the road to midnight snacks that can plague you for one or two years. By feeding the baby, you actually reinforce the act of awakening during the night for food. Before long, a habit sets in that can drive you mad. The best thing to do is go to your baby, see what's the matter, correct it if possible, and go back to bed. Don't lavish tenderness unless you feel your child truly needs it. When these rare times occur, give all the love and support you can. But the main point is: if you, your wife, and your child all sleep through the night on a regular basis, you will all be the happier for it. If you help your child establish regular sleep habits at a young age, you are giving your whole family, most of all your child, a gift for life.

Thumb sucking.

Thumb sucking in bed is not really a problem, but parents often feel it is. If it bothers you, try giving your baby a pacifier instead.

Don't put your baby to sleep with a bottle of milk or juice.

While sucking on the bottle may calm your baby, the milk or juice left in your baby's mouth can cause decay in your baby's first teeth. If your baby has this habit, substitute water in the bottle. If necessary, gradually dilute the milk or juice until there is only water left.

Approximate age range: 6 to 9 months

NAPPING

Naps are an important part of the day for babies this age, who usually take one nap in the morning and one in the afternoon. Naptime routines are appreciated by babies, so no matter where you are with your baby or what you are doing, give your baby a chance to sleep at naptime. Routines help children function. Similarly, babies like naptime rituals, such as a song by you or perhaps just a winding up of a musical mobile overhead. But don't wind up a mobile that's too exciting. A slow-moving, soothing mobile is best for naptime. Make your naptime routines short and sweet. Overstimulating your baby with games and silly chants will be counterproductive. Save those for when Baby wakes up. As babies grow, they sleep less at naptime.

Approximate age range: 6 to 9 months

TOILETING

You may notice that your baby is now beginning to eliminate on a more scheduled basis. For example, you may notice that your baby will stay dry for an hour or so. While you can't make plans on the basis of these observations, you can get a sense of how your baby is maturing. But there's still a long way to go before toilet training begins.

An easy way to carry diapers and other baby supplies with you when you're out.

If you're taking your child out in a backpack and don't want to be bothered carrying a diaper bag, try a waist pack. Pack the waist pack with a diaper, a bottle, some teething biscuits, small rattles, a few wipes, a twist tie, and an empty plastic bag (the last two for the used diaper).

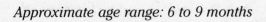

Approximate age range: 6 to 9 months

THE BEST GAME FOR THE CHANGING TABLE

Babies learn about their fingers, hands, arms, toes, feet, and legs by moving them, watching them, and tasting them. You can add to the delight by wiggling your baby's toes and chanting the famous Mother Goose rhyme "This Little Piggy." In case you forget the words, here they are:

"This Little Pig" (or Piggy)

This little pig went to market,
This little pig stayed home,
This little pig had roast beef,
This little pig had none,
And this little pig cried Wee, wee, wee,
All the way home.

Approximate age range: 6 to 9 months

BATH TIME PROBLEMS?

What to do if your baby hates to take a bath.

1. Make sure the water isn't too cold or too hot. Test it with your elbow, which is more sensitive to hot water than your hands.

2. Change your procedures. Try the bath in a different place, in a different way, and perhaps at a different time of day. You might even try having someone different give the baby a bath. This new person could be you!

3. Make the bath fun. Have a bath toy handy. Let your baby splash.

4. Skip the shampoo, if that's the problem. Just wash the head with a warm, soapy washcloth for now. Hold the baby's head back so that soap can't drip into the eyes.

5. Make the bath a quickie. But in your haste, be careful. Keep a close watch and a secure grip on your baby.

6. If all else fails, skip the entire bath. Babies usually don't get that dirty. Give your baby a sponge bath for a few days and then try again. By that time, your baby's bath fears may have abated.

Approximate age range: 6 to 9 months

A GREAT BATH TIME SONG

Make up a variation of "Row, Row, Row Your Boat."

Sing the tune with the regular words as you are getting your baby ready for the bath; then, as you are washing various body parts, make up different verses to correspond. The result is good for language development as well as for making bath time pleasant.

Wash, wash, wash your hands,
Gently down the stream,
Merrily, merrily,
Merrily, merrily,
Life is but a dream.

Wash, wash, wash your face,
Gently down the stream,
Merrily, merrily,
Merrily, merrily,
Life is but a dream.

Wash, wash, wash your feet,
Gently down the stream,
Merrily, merrily,
Merrily, merrily,
Life is but a dream.

Wash, wash, wash your tummy,
Gently down the stream,
Merrily, merrily,
Merrily, merrily,
Life is but a dream.

Wash, wash, wash your back,
Gently down the stream,
Merrily, merrily,
Merrily, merrily,
Life is but a dream.

Approximate age range: 6 to 9 months

DRESSING GAMES & SONGS

Continue, when you have time, to play games with your baby as you are getting him or her dressed. Make up these games to fit your baby's abilities and interests. Here are some possibilities:

May I have it?

Since your baby is learning how to hold things, give your baby the next article of clothing you are going to put on him or her. When you are ready, ask, "May I have it?" Be ready to substitute the next item of clothing for the one you are taking.

This is the way we put on the shirt.

Remember the song "Here We Go Round the Mulberry Bush"? The tune and words adapt well to any process you and your child are involved with. For example, when you are dressing your child, you might sing:

This is the way we put on the shirt/ Put on the shirt/ Put on the shirt,
This is the way we put on the shirt/ As we dress the baby.

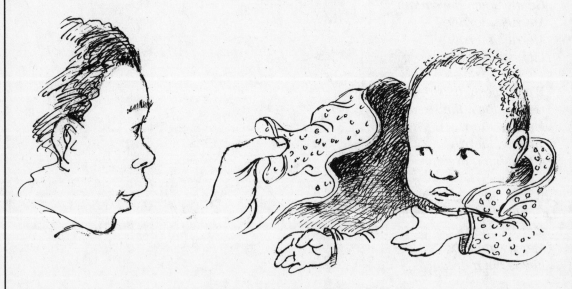

Approximate age range: 6 to 9 months

COMFORTABLE CLOTHING

As your baby grows, clothing may become too tight and too small. Pajamas with feet may no longer fit. Sometimes you can cut the feet off, and the pj's will fit a little longer. Otherwise, put outgrown clothing aside to save for another baby or give away to others. Keep on the lookout for good sources of hand-me-downs. Used baby clothes are not only free or inexpensive, but they also have a nice, soft, comfortable feel to them. Baby shoes are not yet really necessary, but booties and sneakers are fine, as long as they fit properly.

Approximate age range: 6 to 9 months

WHAT CAN BABY HEAR NOW?

Sound game.

Babies are learning to turn toward sounds like the dog barking, the phone ringing, and the vacuum cleaner going. To help your baby develop the ability to turn toward a sound and locate its source, you can play a simple game. Ring a bell or shake a rattle off to the side where your baby isn't looking. When he or she turns to the noise, reward your baby with an enthusiastic cheer, such as, "You found the bell!" This is a good game to teach older brothers and sisters to play with the baby.

When you call babies this age by name, they will turn toward your voice, which they recognize (though they may not recognize their names yet) and try to make eye contact. They like it if you make eye contact back and carry on a little conversation—this kind of auditory stimulation is fun for babies, and they will try to respond with their own auditory repertoire of burbles and coos.

Approximate age range: 6 to 9 months

WHAT CAN BABY SEE NOW?

When they were younger, babies didn't have peripheral vision. Now they do. When they were younger, they couldn't see small things well. Now they can. They gradually develop the ability to see little crumbs of food and may try to pick them up. Their favorite things to watch are their own hands and people.

Object permanence.

Babies will now look briefly to see something that's dropped out of view. If they drop a rattle, they may look down. If you take a toy away, they may look to see where you put it. What they are gradually learning is that objects they see have permanence; that is, they don't disappear just because Baby can't see them anymore. This is a major intellectual leap for Baby; it doesn't happen all at once. Disappearance games, such as peek-a-boo, stimulate the process.

Peek-a-boo!

Peek-a-boo gives babies the opportunity to play with the idea that just because they can't see you (because you have your hands over your face) doesn't mean you aren't there. This game is a big hit for months and months because the underlying concept is a challenging one for babies. They like to play the game, too—imitating the motion of covering their face with their hands.

Approximate age range: 6 to 9 months

A More Exciting and More Dangerous World

Now that they can pick up things and hold on to them better, babies feel a measure of control over their world, and consequently they can amuse themselves more. One of their favorite things to do is pick up things and stick them in their mouths. They do this to taste things and also to relieve aching gums. This activity makes the world infinitely more interesting to babies, but also more dangerous. Always be aware of what's around that could pose a threat to your curious baby. And be aware, too, of safe household things that your baby can pick up and hold. Give them to your baby to explore.

Great things for baby to hold.

Rattles
Teething toys
Cold teething toys
Bagels (try frozen ones)
Teething biscuits

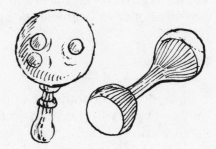

Dangerous things for baby to hold.

Marbles
Pennies
Tiny toys
Buttons
Pebbles
Nuts
Dead bugs
Pills
Mothballs
Balloons

Keep an alert eye out for small things that babies can choke on, as well as things that are poisonous. Ask your pediatrician what to do if your baby chokes on something and what to do if your baby swallows something poisonous. Know these procedures ahead of time. Don't wait until it's too late. If there is an infant CPR course offered in your area, consider taking it.

Approximate age range: 6 to 9 months

REACHING & GRASPING CAUTIONS

Now that babies know how much fun it is to hold on to something, they want to hold on to more and more things. This desire inspires them to survey the environment, reach out, and grasp fascinating things, such as hair, earrings, spoons, and jewelry. This behavior can be annoying to you, unless you understand what's going on and find solutions to the problem. One solution is to get used to your baby clutching your beard. Another is to find something better for your baby to grasp and make up another grasping game.

Reaching and grasping game.

Hold something in front of your baby. As your baby reaches for it, pull it slightly away. Do this only as long as your baby is having fun stretching and reaching. Reward your baby by giving it to the baby. Talk to your baby as you're playing this game. Be as silly and goofy, if you want.

Approximate age range: 6 to 9 months

TWO GREAT DISCOVERIES

It's fascinating to observe babies in the process of discovering what their hands can do. You can't really teach your baby these skills, but you can make sure that your baby has things to hold and manipulate.

#1
How to Turn Things Over in Your Hand

Small wooden blocks or plastic cubes with various pictures and letters printed on them are interesting objects for babies to hold, not because the letters and pictures teach babies to read, but because the blocks change as babies turn them over.

As babies teach themselves to turn the blocks over in their hands, which they will do in time, they are rewarded by the different graphics, a payoff that plain color blocks cannot deliver.

Approximate age range: 6 to 9 months

#2
How to Pick Up Peas and Carrots with Your Fingers

Babies are fascinated to discover how to use their thumb and finger as tweezers to pick up small things. One way to feed a baby who likes to pick up small things is to put slices and pieces of soft food on the high chair tray. The food needs to be appropriate for this age and manner of feeding. Sliced banana, sliced cooked carrots, peas, and cooked macaroni work well.   Be sure to use a bib, and be prepared to clean up afterward because Baby can be messy! Caution: babies can pick up small unsafe things with their fingers, too, so be alert.

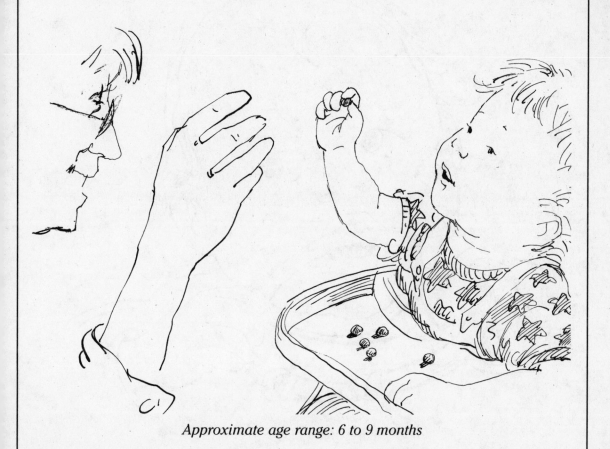

Approximate age range: 6 to 9 months

BABY'S FIRST FOUR TEETH

Babies usually get their first teeth between six and nine months, most often around the seventh month. But babies differ—some getting their first tooth at four months and others as late as twelve months. By the end of the first year most babies have four to eight teeth.

The first teeth are usually the two front bottom teeth, followed by the two front top teeth. Then two more teeth appear on top, followed by two more teeth on the bottom. The teeth may be a little crooked, but don't worry. When the teeth are fully erupted, the natural pressures of the musculature of the lips and the tongue usually align them. Boys' teeth usually erupt slightly earlier than girls.

Approximate age range: 6 to 9 months

PROBLEMS WITH TEETHING

Teething is not always painful; but when it is, babies seem to like something hard, such as a teething biscuit or a teething toy, to bite down on. They also seem to get relief from biting and sucking on cold objects, such as a small piece of ice wrapped in a clean cloth, a frozen damp washcloth, or an unpointy fat frozen carrot. Make sure that the carrot is thick enough that your baby can't bite pieces off and possibly choke on them. Some babies like you to rub on their gums with your finger. If your baby seems in great pain from teething, consult your pediatrician for advice.

Approximate age range: 6 to 9 months

THE PLEASURES (AND DANGERS) OF POKING

Babies this age like to poke things. There are two interesting aspects to this activity. One, babies like the way it feels to poke things; and, two, they like to observe what happens. Some things are hard and boring to poke because nothing happens. But other things are much more fun.

Fun things to poke.

Food

A damp, rolled-up washcloth

A wet sponge

A beanbag

Make sure that whatever you give babies to poke is safe for them to pick up and put in their mouths, which is what they'll inevitably do.

Poking and scratching.

Babies have little fingers that can get in little spaces. They like, for example, to poke their fingers into grungy spaces between floorboards and scratch around. If there's any old gooey food and dirt in there, Baby's little finger will get it, hold it up, look at it with fascination, and then pop it in the mouth. The moral is: watch your child. Always know what your child is doing when loose on the floor.

Poking at electrical outlets.

Babies on the floor may creep over to electrical outlets, notice the little holes in them, stick their fingers or an object in, and get a shock. To prevent this, cover all outlets within their reach with safety plugs, which are widely available in hardware and home supply stores.

Approximate age range: 6 to 9 months

"Stop Poking Me!"

If your baby likes to poke, watch out for your eyes. And teach your baby's brothers and sisters to watch out for theirs, too. Siblings may get very angry when Baby pokes them. Explain that Baby is learning new things to do with fingers and doesn't mean to cause harm. Teach older children to give Baby something else to poke and say, "You can't poke me, but you can poke this...See? Poke, poke, poke!"

Approximate age range: 6 to 9 months

SQUEEZING THINGS

Babies this age also learn how to squeeze things with their hands. The best toys for squeezing are ones that make a noise or do something when you squeeze them. Soft little rubber animals that squeak or moo are very popular. Make sure they are safe for baby to mouth.

Approximate age range: 6 to 9 months

SHAKING THINGS

Rattles continue to be interesting. Since they are usually inexpensive, buy new ones to substitute for old ones your baby is used to. You can also make new shaking toys.

Great homemade shaking toys.

• A film can with a bell inside. Make sure your child can't open it.

• A metal Band-Aid box with pebbles inside. Tape the top tightly so that your baby can't open the box. Later, when your baby is old enough to understand not to eat the contents, you and your child can experiment with different items to put in the box. Then, you won't have to tape the box shut, but for now, do.

• A small transparent bottle with a few buttons inside. Old pill bottles* are good. Make sure the top is impossible for the baby to open. Transparent shakers are good because babies can see what's inside them and make the connection between the sound and the sound maker. *Caution: store all pill bottles and other medicine on high shelves that your baby cannot reach now and throughout childhood.*

Double-check to make sure that homemade toys are safe.

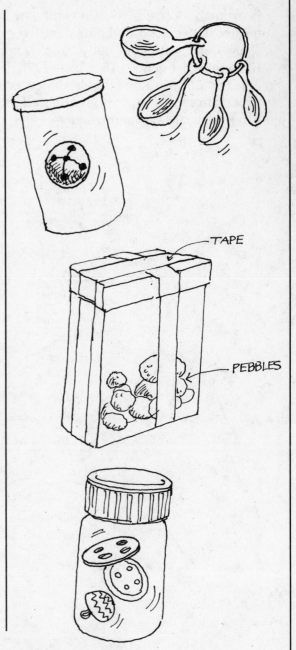

TAPE

PEBBLES

Approximate age range: 6 to 9 months

Bringing Both Hands Together

Bringing both hands together willingly is a neat trick that babies usually
master between six and nine months of age. You can help by starting to play
"Pat-a-Cake" with your baby, holding your baby's hands in yours and clapping
them together gently. (See page 172.) It will take a while for your baby to be
able to clap without your assistance, so don't be overly ambitious in your
expectations. Accept your baby's efforts as they are and have confidence that
progress is always being made—even though you can't necessarily see it.

Approximate age range: 6 to 9 months

3/6/06

Dear Jer + Helen,

This care package has a little of this + that.

It started because I wanted to do more for your birthday, Helen and it grew from there. I hope you enjoy it – don't try to figure it out ☺

Dad + I enjoyed having you here last week-end.

And I think we're still taking in the news of your baby. We both agree you will be wonderful parents + we're so looking forward to this very special

BABIES AT WORK:
HOLDING SOMETHING WITH BOTH HANDS

Babies at this age continue to work hard on various hand skills. As seen on previous pages, they work on poking, squeezing, shaking, and bringing their hands together. And now here comes a new challenge: holding something with both hands. Not easy! It takes a lot of practice and a growing sense of intention. What may seem like meaningless playing and fiddling with a toy to you is, for your baby, a hard day's work at the office.

Approximate age range: 6 to 9 months

HEADS UP SITTING—WITH HELP

At six months most babies will try to sit up alone and fail; by nine months most will be successful. Without pushing your child, you can help him or her practice by putting your baby in safe sitting places, such as your lap or on a soft rug on the floor. Prop pillows around your baby on the floor for support and safety's sake. At first your baby will only be able to sit for a minute or two. This time will eventually lengthen. Don't leave a baby who can't sit up alone. Be there to help when your baby falls over and to pick up your baby when it's time for sitting practice to be over.

Approximate age range: 6 to 9 months

STRONGER LEGS

Babies this age strengthen their leg muscles by lying on their backs and kicking at the air and also by standing on your lap and bouncing on your legs.

Some babies this age start pulling themselves up on things. They may appear to be ready to stand alone and even walk, but they aren't. They need to be supported or to hold on to someone or something. Stay close to catch them when they fall.

"With the first child, I had to train myself not to be a nervous father," says a father of four. "After that, it got easier. I guess I learned to anticipate danger without thinking too much about it. Keeping children safe becomes second nature after a while."

VERY EARLY WALKING

Most babies learn to walk between twelve and fourteen months of age, but some babies learn to walk before they are one year old, some as early as seven or eight months. Such children do this on their own—not as the result of parental intervention. So relax, and don't get competitive about when your child learns to walk.

Approximate age range: 6 to 9 months

THE IMPORTANCE OF KICKING AT THINGS

Babies lying on their backs love to have objects hanging from a mobile or baby floor gym to kick at. As they kick, they make the objects move and make noise. Why does this remain important? Because through such experiences, babies continue to develop the all-important sense that they can make things happen in the world.

Approximate age range: 6 to 9 months

Prison Pen or Playpen?

Playpens can be like prisons to babies left in them for too long. Even if left in them for a short time, wide-awake babies can get awfully bored if there is nothing to do in the playpen. But playpens can also be great mini-environments for babies and very helpful to parents who need a break to make a phone call, write a letter, or just rest for a while.

How to make a playpen fun and safe.

Change the toys in it frequently. Make sure they are appropriate for the activities your child is currently interested in. Wash the playpen pad frequently so that it remains clean; and, occasionally, wash the toys in the playpen. Place the playpen in different, interesting places so that baby has different views to look at. Most of all, don't expect your baby to stay in the playpen too long. A half an hour is a long time. Make sure the playpen is sturdy and poses no hazards to your baby.

Approximate age range: 6 to 9 months

STOMACH GYMNASTICS

Babies continue their self-created and self-imposed exercise program. Adults should be so motivated! All you need to do to help your baby is put him or her down on the tummy. Your baby, if wide-awake and feeling fine, will most likely take it from there. If you want to do something, get down on your tummy, too, and try copying your baby's motions.

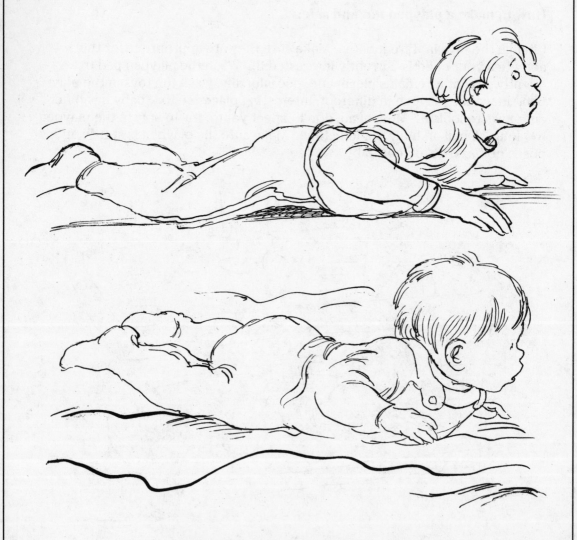

Approximate age range: 6 to 9 months

PUSH-UPS

Babies get better and better at their push-ups. They are able to lift more of their bodies off the ground now. You can sense their determination to get up on their knees and crawl, even though they don't yet have the strength and coordination. The urge to crawl comes from within—babies will keep practicing precrawling skills they need until they can put them all together and actually get somewhere.

Approximate age range: 6 to 9 months

CREEPERS AND WIGGLERS

Before babies crawl, an act that involves lifting their tummies off the ground, they devise ways to creep, that is, to get around without lifting their tummies at all or only partially. First, most of them wiggle and squirm from one place to another. Then they creep and scoot around ingeniously, pulling with their arms and pushing with their legs. They may go forward, backward, or in a circle. All this movement is wonderful exercise, so put your baby down regularly on the floor for precrawling practice. If you like, you can encourage your baby to move forward by holding a toy out or by putting a toy on the ground just out of reach.

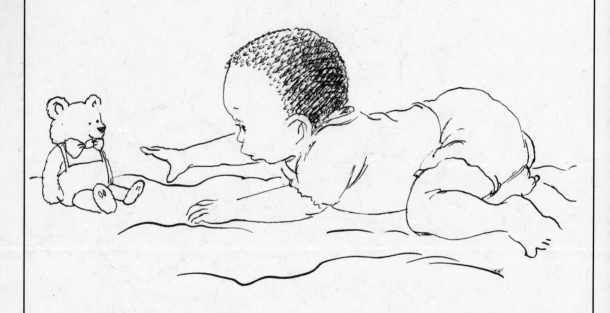

Some babies don't creep, they just rock themselves back and forth without going anywhere. If your baby can't or doesn't move around much yet, don't assume you can leave him or her alone. You need to keep your eye always on your precrawler because you never know when he or she is going to take off!

Approximate age range: 6 to 9 months

ATTEMPTS TO STAND AND WALK

Babies this age may try to stand and walk with your help, but their leg muscles are usually not strong enough to support them for very long, and they don't know how to sit down. So hold on tight. When you see your baby's legs buckle, catch your baby up in your arms. Respect your baby's personal timetable, and don't push walking before your baby is ready.

Approximate age range: 6 to 9 months

TURNING OVER

Babies this age like to practice rolling over. Usually, they go from stomach to back and then they learn to go the other way. (See page 60.) Whichever, rolling over is great exercise. You can encourage it by playing rolling over games on the changing table. Watch that your baby doesn't roll off; this can happen quickly!

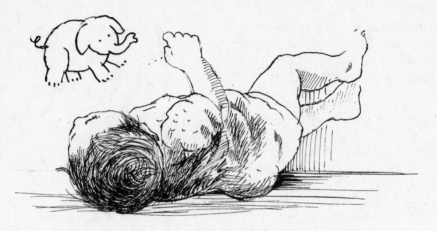

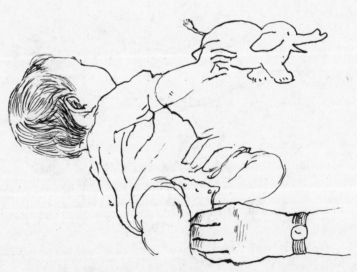

Approximate age range: 6 to 9 months

How to Change a Squiggly Baby

While rolling over is developmentally beneficial and fun for Baby, it can be a pain for you if you are trying to change your baby quickly. You might think your baby is deliberately trying to annoy you. But that's not so. Your baby is just having fun. If you have no time for rollover games, give your baby a toy. Temporarily distracted, your baby will hold still for moment while you get the diaper on. It's a good idea to have a changing selection of toys handy when changing a squiggly baby. Old baby rattles that your baby may have outgrown work fine. Also, when you're out, car keys.

Approximate age range: 6 to 9 months

PAIN AND SORROW

By now your baby has experienced many unpleasant emotions—hunger, pain, exhaustion, fear, disgust, mild anger, rage, and so on. You and others have been there to comfort and soothe; but, as you know, life is not perfect, and it's not always easy to calm a crying baby. You can hope that the happy experiences in your baby's life far outnumber the unhappy ones and give your child the basis for developing a positive and hopeful, yet realistic, outlook on life.

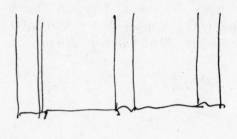

Approximate age range: 6 to 9 months

JOY AND ECSTASY

Babies this age may be absolutely thrilled when you come into their vision to greet them in the morning or after a nap. They recognize you now as a trust-worthy, loving person, but more than that—you are so much fun! You hug, cuddle, coo, sing, cheer, and lift them high into the air. You can be the most exciting person in the world when you reach down into the crib and pick your baby up. What could be better! The ability to take enthusiastic pleasure in your loved ones is not an instinct—it is a precious talent your lucky baby is learning from you.

Approximate age range: 6 to 9 months

AMUSING ONESELF WITH SOUNDS

Babies this age may be content to lie in a crib or playpen and babble to themselves. Sometimes, especially, when you are trying to catch a few more minutes of sleep in the morning or finish something you're doing, it makes sense to let babies continue to babble happily. When babies become bored with their babblings, they will let you know. They may even have figured out by now how to shout with sounds that seem like words! And, being a parent, you might be able to figure out what the shouts means: *Hey, Dada! Come here! Get me up! Now!*

Approximate age range: 6 to 9 months

TWO-WAY BABBLING

Sometimes it makes sense to go over to a happily babbling baby and babble back. This is, after all, one of the most effective ways we teach babies to communicate. They make a sound, we make the same sound. We transform their one-way efforts into two-way conversation, and they like that. They like knowing that their sounds have an effect on us—and that our sounds have an effect on them.

Approximate age range: 6 to 9 months

PROPER NOUNS...

Babies now not only begin to recognize their own names being called; they also begin to recognize others by name, too. They may enjoy playing name games, which are among the first games people invent to play with babies. In such games, older people, including siblings, ask repeated questions such as *Where's Mommy? Is that Mommy?* The lucky babies who look at Mommy are rewarded with a chorus of enthusiastic praise—*Yes, that's Mommy. Mommy! That's Mommy! Mommy! Mommy!* Thus, a pleasurable—and very effective—language education process is begun for the benefit of your child.

Approximate age range: 6 to 9 months

...And Adjectives

When you're with your baby, talk casually about the qualities of things your baby experiences. "The cat is soft," you might say as you hold your baby's hand and together pet the cat. Babies, of course, are not yet able to use adjectives themselves, but your use of them helps them build a foundation for later usage. Here are some of the adjectives you might use:

The bottle is warm.

The towel is fuzzy.

The banana is white.

THIS GRASS IS TICKLY...

...ICKY...

Approximate age range: 6 to 9 months

THE STUDY OF SPEECH

Babies often reach out and touch the lips of people talking to them. They are fascinated by the ways lips move and make sounds. When this happens you might say, "Yes, you can feel my lips moving. They help me make different sounds."

Make different sounds for your baby to listen to, watch, and feel. Show off all the different sounds you can make: mmmmm, ba-ba-ba-ba, pa-pa-pa-pa, la-la-la-la, and so on. Your baby may try to imitate you. Then, you can touch your baby's lips and say, "You make sounds with your lips, too." This is also a good conversation to carry on in front of the mirror.

Approximate age range: 6 to 9 months

You Are the Teacher

Professor Dad, please don't be boring, and don't get tense. Don't talk so much that your baby wishes you would shut up. Language learning should be natural and fun. All you really have to do to be a great teacher for your child is be an interested conversationalist, a good listener, and a friendly fellow traveler. Go out in the world together.

"I take my son to the hardware store and the flea market," says a thirty-something father, "but the Nebraska football game was a little too much for him. He was shocked by the noise of the crowd. I guess I won't be able to teach him about the quarterback sneak for a few more years."

Approximate age range: 6 to 9 months

MORE THAN CRYING

Infants cry to express their needs, but older baby develop a wider repertoire of ways to express their negative feelings. They can frown, grunt, smirk, and shout out their anger. Their negative expressions will frustrate you at times, but when they do, think back to how much more frustrating it was when they were younger and you didn't know what was wrong. Now, chances are you know. You can tell, most of the time, when your baby is sad, afraid, hungry, hurt, or just plain furious. And knowing what's wrong makes it a little easier to come up with appropriate solutions.

Approximate age range: 6 to 9 months

YOU ARE THE TRANSLATOR

Because you know your baby, you are one of the most able adults to explain your baby to the outside world. If you see a sibling, baby-sitter, or day-care worker misinterpreting your baby's attempts to communicate, speak up. Explain what you think your baby is trying to get across. Don't be shy. At the same time, if you think someone else is understanding your baby better than you, ask what's happening. Be ready to learn so that you can be a better parent. People who have raised children or who care for babies professionally can be very wise; if it helps, let them translate your baby's actions for you.

Approximate age range: 6 to 9 months

BABY'S FIRST WORDS

The first words that babies speak are the names they learn for the people and most important objects in their world. Your job is to respond enthusiastically, an easy task, since first words are such an exciting development. "My favorite memory of my daughter as a baby," says one father, "is when she first called me Papa. At last our relationship was not blob to blob, but rather person to person, daughter to father."

Approximate age range: 6 to 9 months

FIRST WORDS AROUND THE WORLD

It is not a coincidence that around the world babies' first words feature the initial consonants of *b*, *p*, and *d*. The sounds of these letters are easy for babies to pronounce. Here's how *Father* is said by babies in various countries:

English: *Dada or Daddy*
Spanish: *Papa*
Russian: *Papa*
Italian: *Babbo*
Chinese: *Ba*

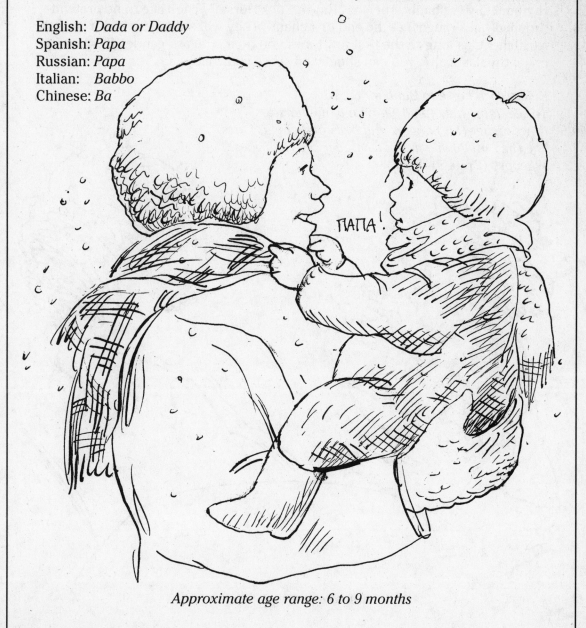

Approximate age range: 6 to 9 months

Rhythm...

Babies like rhythm more than ever now. They like to be bounced, jiggled, and jounced to music. They like to be rocked in your arms or on your hips while you're talking to a neighbor. They like to sit on your knee and be bounced rhythmically to chants, such as "Ride a Cock Horse." They like to be pretend-dropped (and caught) at the end of a chant. They will anticipate the drop with excitement, as long as the first few times you do it, you are gentle. If you start too enthusiastically, you can shock and scare your baby.

Ride a cock horse to Banbury Cross,
To see a fine lady (gent) upon a white horse;
Rings on her (his) fingers and bells on her (his) toes,
She (he) shall have music wherever she (he) goes.
Whoops! (Pretend-drop.)

Approximate age range: 6 to 9 months

...And Music

Babies continue to love to be sung to. So, if you do sing (and really—everybody does), indulge yourself and your baby. If you don't like to sing, you might play your favorite music or perhaps tapes of baby lullabies and children's songs. While listening to tapes in the car, both you and your baby can get to learn new songs. Your baby may not seem to be old enough yet to enjoy them, but the tunes are in the air, and your baby is absorbing them.

Approximate age range: 6 to 9 months

POSITIVE REINFORCEMENT

If you like something your baby does or says, show your pleasure. Since your baby likes to please you, he or she will probably try to do the same thing again. Such positive reinforcement is a powerful incentive for your baby.

Approximate age range: 6 to 9 months

LEARNING ABOUT NO-NO'S

If you don't like something your baby does (like hitting a sibling or reaching for a pan on the stove), show your displeasure by simply and firmly saying, "No hitting" or "Hot!" while simultaneously moving the baby away from the sibling or stove. Don't make a big deal of it; negative reinforcement does not require shouting and violence. You don't need to hit your baby. Hitting can harm your baby physically and destroy the trust you have built up. When your baby is around nine months, you can start explaining in simple language why certain actions and things are no-no's. Before that, just say no with a clear, firm voice and show you mean it with clear, firm actions.

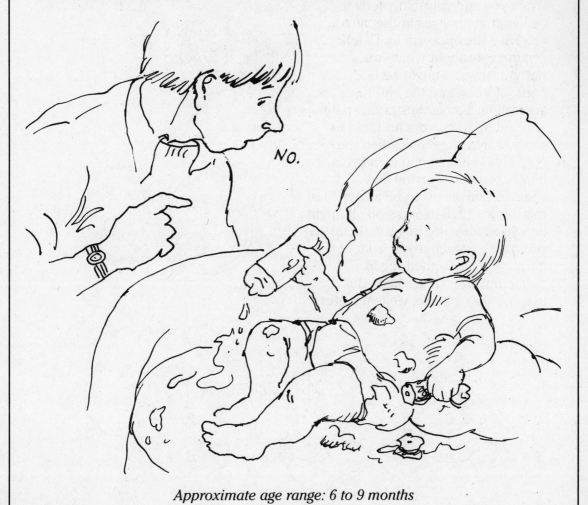

Approximate age range: 6 to 9 months

THE FASCINATION OF MIRRORS

Mirrors are great for babies because they are responsive, that is, the image in the mirror responds when babies move. Babies are intrigued by this and can learn a lot just by watching themselves in a mirror. Small, safe mirror toys are made to hang in cribs and playpens. Safe baby mirrors can also be found in toys, such as rattles and busy boxes.

Looking in the mirror with your baby.

When you and your baby look together at yourselves in the mirror, you have the opportunity to talk comfortably about what you see. Natural subjects might be body parts, clothes, and the emotions you are feeling. Sometimes crying babies are held up to mirrors and told to see how ugly they look when they cry. This is not a good idea because babies can't help crying and shouldn't be taught to be ashamed of this mode of self-expression. It might be a good idea, on the other hand, to stand with a sad baby in front of the mirror and say something like, "Sometimes we all feel sad. But usually, after a while, we feel better."

Approximate age range: 6 to 9 months

132

STRANGER ANXIETY

As babies relate more and more to you and other familiar people in their lives, they learn to differentiate between people they know and people they don't know. The difference doesn't matter to some babies, who will go happily into a friendly stranger's arms. But other babies experience anxiety when handed to a stranger, no matter how welcoming the stranger is. This poses a problem when a new baby-sitter or a relative who rarely visits wants to hold your baby.

To solve the problem, first understand your baby's point of view. Sit down with your baby next to the stranger. Give the stranger an interesting toy and then carry on a normal conversation about the child, the toy, or something else. Sooner or later, your baby will manifest an interest in the toy that can lead to interaction with the stranger. Through activities like this, if you don't push it, barriers will break down and the stranger will soon become a friend. It may take only a few minutes or it can take a few days. If your baby has stranger anxiety and you're hiring a new full-time baby-sitter, plan to have her visit until the stranger anxiety fades.

Approximate age range: 6 to 9 months

BABIES & PATIENCE

For children, patience is a hard-won trait, learned very, very gradually over all their years of childhood, including adolescence. Babies don't have much patience, but they develop the trait incrementally as they mature. There are some wise things you can do to help your baby avoid losing patience. Since patience is not a strong point, it makes sense to prevent situations in which you end up wishing your baby had more of it.

Appetizers prevent hunger fits.

You can help your child wait for supper by giving him or her an appetizer, such as a teething biscuit or banana slices.

Solve the toy retrieval problem.

Babies eventually learn to throw and release objects they are holding in their hands. This is a complex skill that is fun for them to practice. The only trouble is that when someone doesn't fetch what Baby throws, Baby gets mad. You may be able to teach another child in the family to fetch for Baby or engage grandparents to do the job. Some grandparents manifest admirable patience in this respect. You can also leash toys to high chairs and cribs so that baby can reel the toys back in. But make sure the leashes are safe and that there's no way that Baby could get caught in them or strangle in them.

Approximate age range: 6 to 9 months

FATHERS & PATIENCE

Fathers, mothers, caregivers, and baby-sitters all lose their patience with babies from time to time. Everyone who takes care of children experiences occasional extreme frustration. When you feel yourself on the verge of losing your temper, tell yourself to keep cool. If another grown-up is present, ask for relief. When your wife is losing it, help her calm down by taking the baby and giving her some relief. Realize others have felt exactly the same way about their adorable but infuriating children. Feeling angry is not wrong; hurting your child is. If possible, summon your sense of humor to help you gain perspective. The following stories, told by two separate fathers, are true. They learned to laugh at their mishaps; so can you.

"My daughter was smashing banana all over the high chair tray and then all over her face. She was a mess, and I flipped out. I don't know what came over me, but I took some smashed banana and spread it over my face, shouting, 'Look, does this look nice?' My daughter laughed. A few moments later, I laughed, too."

"I had fed my son. I had changed him. I had burped him. I had rocked him. I had rubbed his back. But still he cried. I sang every lullaby I knew, but nothing worked. I was so exhausted that I couldn't stand another minute of taking care of him. I put him in the crib, and he howled. Suddenly, I gripped the crib rail with both of my hands and shook it. You know what happened? The baby stopped crying. I kept jiggling the crib in a steady motion, and the baby went to sleep. I couldn't believe it. He must have liked that motion."

Approximate age range: 6 to 9 months

CHAPTER FOUR:
9 TO 12 MONTHS

"I always felt criticized by my parents as I grew up," says one father, "and I didn't like it. So I've decided not to be the judge of my daughter. I figure that the best thing to do is to accept her inherent disposition and physical traits. It's not that I have *no* expectations. It's that I hope the ones I have are reasonable and that she will grow up with more confidence than I did."

This chapter will give you general guidelines regarding the development of children between the ages of nine and twelve months. Appreciate the unique way your child is unfolding, matching some of the guidelines but perhaps not others. Be flexible. Your job is to create a world, not of judgment, but of stimulation, acceptance, and love within which your baby will thrive. Your baby is a person, not an acquisition and not a blank slate on which you can record your ideas of the perfect baby. Your baby has a personality all his or her own, and these months will see it blossoming.

Approximate age range: 9 to 12 months

If you feel estranged, it's not too late.

Unfortunately, not all fathers get it the way this father does. Some fathers have withdrawn so much from the parental role by the time their child is nine months old that they don't know how to be with their baby in any way other than supervisory. If you think this might have happened to you, if you find yourself tense and even shy around your child, don't despair. It's not too late. You can do something about it. You can change. First of all, stop thinking about yourself and think, instead, about your child. Second, read the following pages closely. They will tell you what babies in this age group are capable of doing. These months are full of wonder, and babies are now at their cuddly cutest. Understanding their interests and innate goals, you'll find it easier and more fun to take care of them.

Most of all, if you are estranged from your baby, don't give up. Pretend you are a new person come to live in your home, and start a new relationship with your child. Don't expect miracles. Relationships take time. Little by little, day by day, you and your baby will win each other's hearts back.

Approximate age range: 9 to 12 months

DRINKING FROM A CUP

It's a challenge for babies to learn how to handle a cup. They usually start by observing other children using cups and become curious about the activity. Next, they put their hands on a cup held by someone else. And, sooner or later, they try to hold the cup themselves with both hands.

The results can be a little messy, but there are ways to keep the mess down. Hold a towel under the cup. Use a baby cup that has a lid and spout. If you use a regular cup without such a lid, make sure the cup only has a little liquid in it. Some cups have two handles that are easy for babies to clutch. And some cups are weighted at the bottom, which prevents tipping when Baby sets the cup down.

Don't be surprised, or worry, if your baby can't master drinking from a cup. Some babies can't do this until they're almost one and a half years old. Others like the breast or bottle so much that they won't drink from a cup until they're older and consciously decide they want to.

Approximate age range: 9 to 12 months

BREAST, BOTTLE, CUP—
WHICH IS BETTER NOW?

No one way is better. Babies do not have to learn to drink from a cup at this age. They may still be breast-feeding or bottle feeding, which is fine—they can learn to drink from a cup later. But many babies do learn to drink from a cup by the time they are one year old, some making the transition from breast to cup without ever using bottles. The two advantages of cups over bottles are that they are easier to clean and that they give babies a sense of maturity.

Approximate age range: 9 to 12 months

Baby's Diet

More finger foods.

As you add more finger foods to your baby's diet, make sure they are nutritious, easy to chew (and gum), and easy to pick up. Avoid raisins and popcorn as well as small, hard foods like nuts and candies because they can be swallowed whole and possibly cause choking.

Most popular finger foods.

Cheerios
Banana and peach slices
Blueberries and strawberries cut in half (watch to see if Baby is allergic to berries)
Small slices of avocado
Small cubes of tofu
Cooked vegetables, such as peas, diced carrots, asparagus, cauliflower, green beans, zucchini, potatoes and yams
Cubes of soft, diced cheese, such as Velveeta and mozzarella
Cubes of cooked meat
Sliced hot dogs (nutritious type)
Meat on small, strong bones
Strips of french toast
Nutritious cookies
Bite-size pieces of an omelet

Messy?

Yes. Finger foods served on a high chair tray can be messy. Babies are sometimes inclined to mash and fingerpaint with their foods instead of eating them. If you serve finger foods on a plate, you may discover that curious babies are inclined to see what happens if they push the plate off the tray. So, messy, yes—which is why some people put newspaper on the floor around the high chair and why dogs hang around high chairs happily. If you like, use baby dishes with suction cups on the bottom. You can also give your child only a few finger food items at a time. Bibs help. Some bibs have pockets at the bottom that collect drippings.

Foods for spoon feeding.

Baby food with small, soft chunks in it is safe for most babies to eat now—and more interesting. They can use their new teeth to chew and gum the chunks. Offer a little spoon to practice eating with, if your baby has shown interest in this activity.

Lip-licking delicious.

One happy, hygienic note: around this age babies discover that they can lick their lips. Eventually, they'll be able to lick them clean. Demonstrate the behavior with enthusiasm, and watch your baby copy you.

Approximate age range: 9 to 12 months

HIGH CHAIR LIFE

Babies can sit up well now in high chairs. From their perch, they can survey the world and experience it in new ways. For example, they can experience gravity by dropping things, watching them fall, and observing where they land. (If you're tired of retrieving things, tie a few on short strings so Baby can fish them back.)

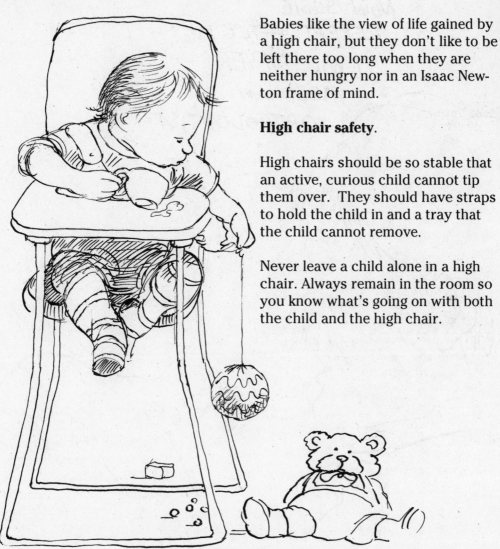

Babies like the view of life gained by a high chair, but they don't like to be left there too long when they are neither hungry nor in an Isaac Newton frame of mind.

High chair safety.

High chairs should be so stable that an active, curious child cannot tip them over. They should have straps to hold the child in and a tray that the child cannot remove.

Never leave a child alone in a high chair. Always remain in the room so you know what's going on with both the child and the high chair.

Approximate age range: 9 to 12 months

TEETH

Babies this age usually have four to six teeth, and their lips and tongue are sufficiently developed for gumming and chewing. They still bite and chew on their toys. But at this age teething is not such a big deal, because teeth hurt less and/or because you are now experienced with the problem.

Approximate age range: 9 to 12 months

TOILETING

Time for toilet training? No, not yet, although some babies have been trained around one year of age. Some would say that it is the parents in most of these cases who are trained, not the children. What happens is that the parents put their child on the potty after being fed and wait for the child to have a bowel movement. If the child is quite regular and responsive, the child may cooperate. However, many babies strongly resist the pressure to "go" on command, and subsequent toileting problems, many of them psychological, can result from early unpleasant experiences. Most pediatricians suggest waiting until children are twenty-two to thirty months old before commencing with toilet training. Best advice? Continue to make the changing of your baby's diapers a time when the two of you can chat in a friendly manner as you get the business over with. Don't react in a negative way to "messes" your child can't help making.

Approximate age range: 9 to 12 months

SLEEPING

Most babies this age continue to need about 13 to 17 hours of sleep a day. They still take a morning nap and an afternoon nap; these naptime hours are part of the 13 to 17 hours. If your baby is cranky and seems tired much of the time, consider his or her schedule. Lack of sleep may be a problem. Going down to sleep at the same time each night and at each naptime helps babies develop a regular sleep pattern. Try to stick to a schedule as much as possible, for everyone's sake. Not all babies need the same amount of sleep. Check with your pediatrician if you have concerns that your baby is not getting enough sleep, no matter what you do.

Approximate age range: 9 to 12 months

LITERARY BEDTIME RITUALS

Soothing bedtime rituals continue to pave the way to peaceful bedtimes. But as your baby matures, you may need to create new routines that work for your older child. Active, rough-and-tumble play before bedtime is not recommended because it winds children up too much and prevents them from falling to sleep. Bedtime stories and books are highly recommended.

Bedtime stories.

These are stories you make up yourself. Put your baby down under the covers, dim or turn off the light, and tell one story in a soft voice. At this age, stories told in repetitive language about animals going to sleep work well. For example, you might say, "All the little kittens are now going to sleep. All the little puppies are now going to sleep. All the little birds are now going to sleep." And so on. End with: "All the little babies are now going to sleep. Good night." Leave. Don't go back unless it's absolutely necessary. Train your child—just one story at each bedtime. The more pleasant you make bedtime, the more likely your child will fall asleep. Don't let your child manipulate you into changing the routine.

Bedtime books.

If you haven't started reading books to your baby, this is a good time to begin. Start with picture books that have clear, simple illustrations and little or no text. (See page 169 for suggested titles.) Children's librarians and clerks in bookstores will also be glad to help you select age-appropriate books.

Approximate age range: 9 to 12 months

BATH TIME

At this age babies are learning to sit up by themselves. (See page 154.) This development brings great satisfaction to babies at bath time because now they can sit in shallow water and play. Most babies love playing with water. They like to splash it, watch it, listen to it, feel it, pour it into containers, and pour it out. Water is a marvelously responsive and flexible toy.

To help your baby enjoy a safe bath time, take a bath with your baby, or sit or kneel on the floor outside the tub within arm's reach. Babies don't need to be entertained now while they're playing in water. Just sit down nearby and provide a few simple bath toys. Enjoy your child's creativity. Bath time can last as long as your baby is warm and contented; when it's over, your baby will let you know.

Bath time can be dangerous.

While sitting-up babies are having a good time by themselves, it's tempting to go off and leave them for a minute. But unattended babies can eat soap, climb out of the tub, and even slip and drown. *Always* stay nearby to supervise.

Great places for a bath.

• Bathtub
• Kitchen sink
• Baby bathtub
• Baby pool

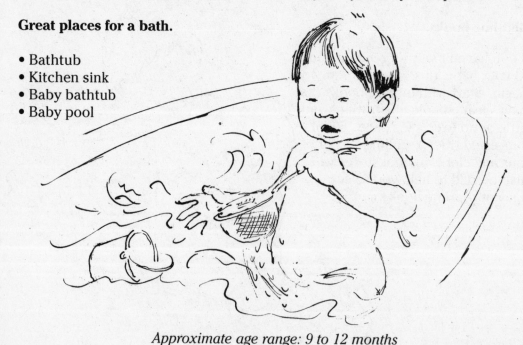

Approximate age range: 9 to 12 months

FAVORITE WATER PLAY TOYS

Babies this age begin to enjoy playing with bath toys that attach to the side of tubs. They also like plastic containers, rubber duckies, boats, other floating bath toys, and miscellaneous plastic toys; make sure all of these are too big to go down the drain. What to do with all the wet bath toys afterward? Store them in a plastic basket at the end of the tub or in a mesh bag hung from a faucet. Safety note: teach your child *not* to turn the faucets.

Approximate age range: 9 to 12 months

DRESSING

At this age babies may begin to be interested in taking off some of their clothes, particularly garments that come off easily. If you have time, let your child help as much as possible when you are getting him or her undressed. Getting dressed and undressed can be planned as an activity in and of itself, not just something that has to be done quickly before something else happens.

Approximate age range: 9 to 12 months

DRESSING CHANTS

If you don't have time to let your child help with getting dressed, you may be able to distract your child from the process with a toy or song. However, if your child wants to be involved with the dressing process, make up a dressing chant. If you're in a hurry, speed up the chant.

Examples of two dressing chants you might make up.

#1:
One, head;
Two, arm;
Three, other arm,
Four, leg;
Five, other leg;
Six, snaps:
Snap, snap, snap.
All done!

#2:
Baby wears socks.
Daddy wears socks.
Mommy wears socks.
Brother wears socks.
Sister wears socks.
Doggie wears socks.
Doggie wears socks?
No! No! No!
Doggie doesn't wear socks.
All done!

ALL DONE!

Approximate age range: 9 to 12 months

HANDLING SMALL OBJECTS

Babies between nine and twelve months of age like to explore their environment, using the hand skills they've worked for months to gain. What they need now is a safe, interesting place in which they can freely explore. They need new small toys to discover as well as old favorites to rediscover. If you have too many toys, try putting some away and bringing them out at intervals. Rotate your baby's toy collection so that your baby always has new items to discover. You don't have to go out and buy *expensive* toys. Inexpensive toys are just as fun—just make sure they are safe. You really don't have to buy anything at all. Plastic containers, plastic jar lids, wooden spoons, measuring cups, and measuring spoons are terrific objects for Baby to explore. Again, just make sure they are safe.

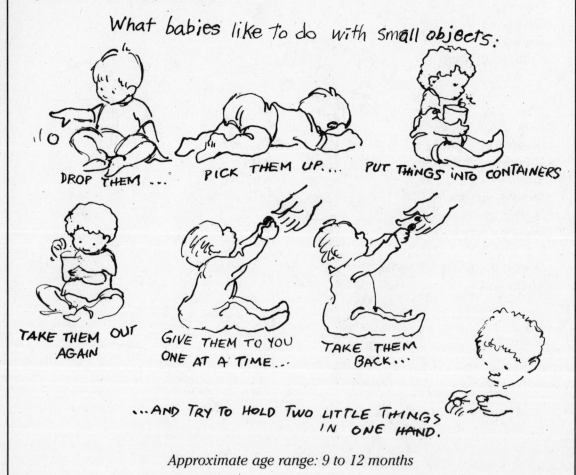

What babies like to do with small objects:

DROP THEM ...   PICK THEM UP....   PUT THINGS INTO CONTAINERS

TAKE THEM OUT AGAIN   GIVE THEM TO YOU ONE AT A TIME...   TAKE THEM BACK...

...AND TRY TO HOLD TWO LITTLE THINGS IN ONE HAND.

Approximate age range: 9 to 12 months

THROWING THINGS

At an earlier age, babies learn to grasp, and then they learn to let go. (See pages 134 and 141.) Now they learn to wind up and really throw things. You can imagine how much fun this is for Baby, but it may not be so much fun for the people who are hit by the wet bagel or who have to pick up the soggy thing from the floor. So, while throwing things may be grand fun for your child and while you can well appreciate the skills involved, you may find that guidance (aka discipline) is in order. Simply say very clearly, "No, you may not throw your bottle (or whatever it is you don't want your baby to throw)." Then, cheerfully give your baby something that *may* be thrown, such as a sponge ball, and say, "But you may throw this ball." With this kind of discipline, everyone comes out a winner.

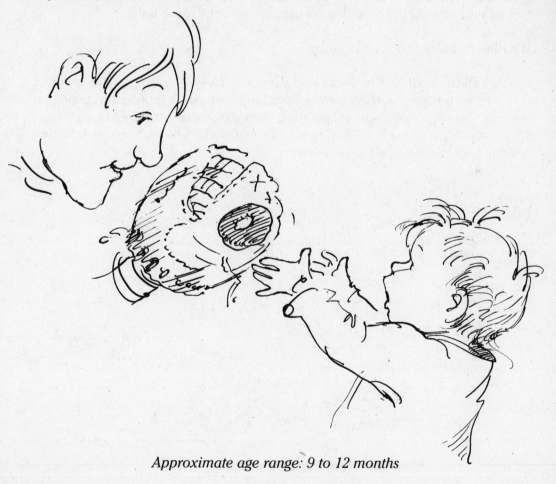

Approximate age range: 9 to 12 months

CRAWLING

The first day babies raise their tummies off the ground and really crawl or develop another equally effective mode of self-locomotion is an important milestone. When this happens, your baby will be able to control life more than ever, traveling while exploring many new and exciting things. This milestone is as thrilling for babies as driving a car is for teenagers.

You're thrilled too, of course, but then you realize the consequences. You too have entered a new phase—your baby has to be watched more than ever! Hazards abound. What are they? Get down on your hands and knees and look around from your baby's point of view. You'll be surprised how much nasty stuff is available on or near the floor that babies can put in their mouths: bobby pins, straight pins, old gum, pieces of thread, dust balls.

It's time to baby proof your home.

Pick up all the stuff on the floors and vacuum. Then, redecorate the lower levels of your home, putting away everything that poses a potential problem. If you are not the one doing these jobs, show appreciation for whoever is. Baby proofing a home is a lot of work. As your baby grows, keep your baby proofing up to date. (See page 161.)

Approximate age range: 9 to 12 months

THE CHALLENGE OF STAIRS

Crawling babies are inevitably drawn to stairs. And good for them for wanting to see if they can crawl up them! For babies, stairs are an appropriate and exciting, albeit dangerous, challenge. But for you, after a while—unless you are in a very, very patient mood, stairs can be quite annoying. The problem is that your baby wants to keep trying to climb them, and you can't leave—not for one second. Not only do you have to provide help, but you also have to prevent your baby from slipping and falling. When you've had enough of stair duty, don't despair. Scoop your baby up and offer an alternative activity, preferably out of sight of the stairs so that Baby will forget about them. The new activity better be a winner or Baby will want to go back to you-know-what.

Approximate age range: 9 to 12 months

SITTING PRETTY

Babies are better sitters now. You no longer need to prop them up with pillows. They sit securely on a solid base and are able to play with things without tipping over. This is the time to introduce safe toys made for sitting babies to play with, such as soft lightweight dolls and stuffed animals, jack-in-the-box-type toys that you punch and something happens, and plastic figures that go with houses (like the Fisher-Price Play Family toys).

Approximate age range: 9 to 12 months

THE ABILITY TO REACH OUT AND SIT BACK UP

Babies have stronger backs now. A while ago, if they leaned forward too far when seated, they couldn't pull themselves back up. Now they can reach out for a toy, grab it, and sit back up in order to play with it. The beauty of this coordination of separate skills is that babies put them together on their own—when they're ready. Your job? To observe the effort and appreciate the outcome and to provide interesting things for your baby to want to reach.

Approximate age range: 9 to 12 months

FROM CRAWLING TO SITTING...

Watch babies this age develop ways to change from one position to another. For example, watch how your baby goes from crawling to sitting. Usually, this involves stopping and giving a little push backward. Your baby's legs are so flexible that they flip from back to front with no trouble.

Approximate age range: 9 to 12 months

...AND FROM SITTING TO CRAWLING

Similarly, watch what your sitting baby does when inspired to crawl. Usually, babies this age figure out how to tip slightly to one side and rock forward as their legs swing around the other side. Though this might be more difficult for big-bellied babies, babies are ingenious at finding solutions to problems.

Approximate age range: 9 to 12 months

STANDING & WALKING WITH HELP

Babies this age begin to pull themselves up on furniture. They would like to stand and walk alone, but usually their legs are not strong enough for them to stand without help. Be sensitive to your baby's desires for standing and walking practice. Provide help and encouragement, but don't push.

Older siblings often enjoy helping babies stand and walk. You may find that you need to caution them to watch the baby carefully. When the baby's legs begin to buckle, the baby should be gently lowered to the ground.

Approximate age range: 9 to 12 months

EARLY WALKERS

Most babies learn to walk between twelve and fourteen months of age, but some babies learn *very* early to walk (see page 107), some learn early (this page), and some learn later. As with all developmental milestones, babies learn when they are ready. They are smart and relaxed enough to compete only against themselves, unless you teach them otherwise.

If you find yourself wanting your baby to walk now, turn to page 209 and read about most babies, who walk between twelve and eighteen months of age. Reading about them will help you feel more at ease when you see another child your baby's age walking.

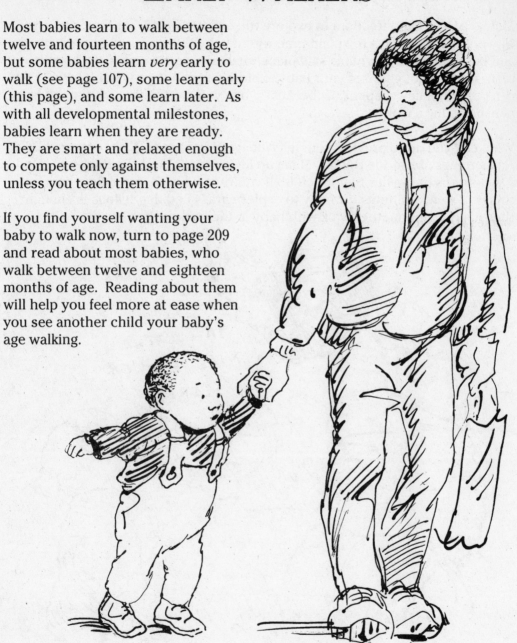

Approximate age range: 9 to 12 months

EXPLORING THE OUTSIDE WORLD

Mobile babies need freedom to explore the outside world— at their own pace. One of the nicest ways to spend time with a baby this age is just to go outside and put your child down in a safe place, such as a yard or park. Of course, no place is safe enough to let your baby explore without your watchful eye. You can't read the newspaper now because while you are reading, your quiet baby may be eating a worm.

What can you do to prevent yourself from getting bored? Talk to your child. Name things. Describe things. Make up little songs about the things you find. Take photos or movies of your child. If you're still bored, put a time limit on things. Twenty minutes for baby to explore grass and dandelions is enough; then it's time for another walk with baby in the backpack.

Approximate age range: 9 to 12 months

MAKING LIFE SAFE FOR BABIES

Is your "baby-proof" home *still* baby-proof?

You may have baby proofed part or all of your home a few months ago. It's time now to check again and make sure it is still safe for your older, more competent baby. Keep in mind that your baby is able to travel farther, reach higher, and pull harder now.

- Remove anything dangerous that your baby could pick up and swallow.

- Cover any dangerous hole that your baby could stick a finger into. You can buy covers and caps for electrical outlets in hardware stores.

- Remove objects, such as vases and plants, that you don't want your baby and your baby's friends to touch.

- Remove breakables and poisonous materials from low cabinets you allow your baby to open. Lock other cabinets with safety locks and latches, available in hardware stores.

- Remove or pad tables that have sharp edges and corners.

- Either remove books and CDs or pack them so tightly together on bookshelves that your baby cannot pull them out.

- Put electrical cords out of reach of babies.

- Remove rocking chairs and other chairs that can pinch or hurt babies.

- Put up gates at the top and bottom of stairs, and in the doorways of rooms that are closed off to your baby.

- When finished, look around. Is there anything left that could endanger your baby? If so, remove it.

- And last, realize that even though your baby is older, that doesn't mean your baby is wiser in regard to safety. Babies this age need to be watched more than ever.

Approximate age range: 9 to 12 months

THE AMAZING LANGUAGE OF BABBLING

Babies continue to babble, making more complex sounds as they grow. Without knowing exactly what they are doing, they practice making the sounds of consonants, particularly *p, b, m, t,* and *d.* Sometimes they combine the consonants with vowel sounds to create syllables. And even more amazing, they may utter these syllables expressively in sentencelike form. When babies do this, they sound as if they are talking in a foreign language! To amuse yourself now and your high school graduate of the future, get out the tape recorder and record your baby's eloquent babbling.

Approximate age range: 9 to 12 months

THE DESIRE TO COMMUNICATE

Babies have such a strong desire to communicate with you that they can't wait until they learn to talk. They want to start now. So, talk with them normally, and listen as they reply in babbles. If you want, babble instead of talking normally. It really doesn't matter, as long as the two of you are communicating on some verbal level.

Notice that your baby may now begin to use language to convey different emotions. Instead of crying, for example, your baby may express anger or shock in a more verbal way. Supply language for your child's sounds and gestures with comments such as "You're mad because you can't get the ball" and "Are you reaching over for a cracker? Here's a cracker."

Approximate age range: 9 to 12 months

LEARNING THE NAMES OF THINGS

Your baby is beginning to learn the names for things. Knowing the names for things doesn't necessarily mean that your baby can say the names. But he or she may know what you mean when you say "doggy," "banana," and "nose." The best way to help your baby learn the names of things is to talk about things casually all the time. You don't have to overdo it. Books with clear, simple pictures also provide good stimulation for naming things.

Most babies this age know the words *Mama* and/or *Dada*. Sometimes they call both parents by one of these names, but in time they learn the difference.

Approximate age range: 9 to 12 months

LISTENING SKILLS

Babies listen better now. When they're playing, they'll stop what they're doing if they hear you call their name. This skill develops more readily if you make a point of using your child's name in conversations.

Babies enjoy listening to people talk because they are studying speech in order to master it themselves. Even if your baby has already eaten, bring him or her in the high chair to the table at family dinnertime so that your baby can hear what's going on. Have a few toys and other small objects for Baby to play with during the meal. Keep in mind that the way your family members talk to one another is the way your child will learn to talk.

Approximate age range: 9 to 12 months

FAVORITE TOYS FOR A ONE-YEAR-OLD

You don't need to buy a lot of toys for your baby, but you and others probably will, regardless of your income level, because buying toys for babies can be fun. But buy wisely; that is, purchase toys that are safe and developmentally appropriate. (See page 173.) Such toys need not be expensive. Some of the most favorite boys for one-year-olds are stacking rings and boxes (see *Caution* below), jack-in-the-box-type toys that pop up when you press a button, light-weight balls of various sizes, and mailbox-type toys that you can put things into (see page 179).

Caution: your baby may ignore directions.

Babies don't always play with toys the way you want them to. The greatest example of this phenomenon is the stacking rings toy. Babies like this toy, but they can't stack the rings in order from largest to smallest the way you can. Furthermore, they don't even want to try. They like to hold the rings, mouth them, and throw them. They may try to put them on the holder but not in the right order. Are babies being willfully obstinate? No. They are acting their age. Not until children are two and a half or three can they stack the rings correctly. Still, the toy is a great one for one-year-olds to play with their way.

Approximate age range: 9 to 12 months

Toy Safety Checklist

Check the toys you buy and that are given to your child by others. Toys for young children should:

- Be too large to be swallowed.

- Have no detachable parts that can be swallowed.

- Have no little parts that can break off and be swallowed.

- Have no sharp edges or points.

- Be well made.

- Not be made of glass or brittle plastic.

- Be nontoxic.

- Have no parts that can pinch fingers or catch hair.

- Have no long cords that could accidentally strangle a young child.

Approximate age range: 9 to 12 months

READING

Babies this age may enjoy sitting on your lap and looking at books. At first, the pleasure is purely sensory: the physical nearness to you, the touch of pages, the sound of your voice. In time, the pleasure becomes intellectual and aesthetic as your baby thinks about the pictures and the content of the text.

When do children learn to read?

Most children read around the age of six, but the impressive ability to look at the letters *c-a-t* and read *cat* is based on book experiences that occur throughout childhood, starting when babies are very young. When your baby touches the fur in *Pat the Bunny*, for example, he or she will begin to enjoy books, and that is the most important first step in learning to read. In other words, most children read at six, but they *start* developing an interest now.

Approximate age range: 9 to 12 months

FIRST BOOKS FOR BABIES

The best books for babies have clear pictures of recognizable things. The pictures may have no text, labels, or a very short text.

Chewable books.

Many books for babies have sturdy cardboard or plastic pages. In addition to reading them to your child, you can put them in the playpen or crib where your child may enjoy looking at them on his or her own. The pages should be nontoxic and be able to survive being gnawed on.

Recommended first books for babies.

Pat the Bunny by Dorothy Kunhardt
Rosemary Wells' *Max* books
Good Morning, Baby by Cheryl Willis Hudson
The Carrot Seed by Ruth Krauss
The First Picture Book by
  Mary Steichen Calderone
What Do Babies Do? by Debby Slier
Books by Dick Bruna
Where's Spot? by Eric Hill
What Is It? by Tana Hoban

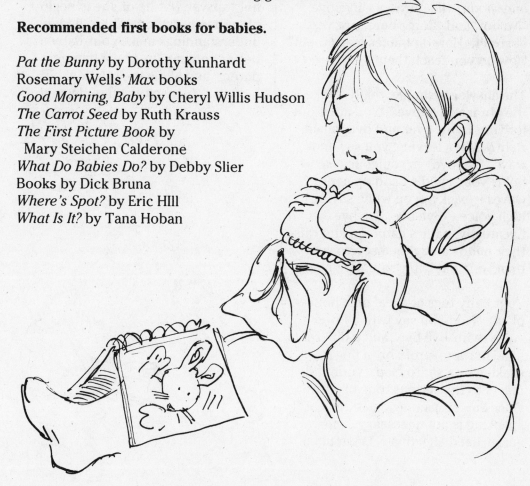

Approximate age range: 9 to 12 months

Bye-bye, No & Come Here: Learning What These Words Mean

Helping your baby grasp the meaning of language continues to be one of the most important jobs of parenthood. Compared to the words *ball* and *spoon,* the phrases "Bye-bye," "No no," and "Come here" are very abstract. How do babies learn them? How do you teach them?

The answer is simple, really. Take the phrase "Bye-bye." You act it out for your baby, over and over again, right? When leaving, you say and wave "Bye-bye" as someone else holds your child's hand up and waves it back to you while saying in a high voice, "Bye-bye, bye-bye." Eventually, babies catch on and raise their hands all by themselves, and then, one day, they say, "Bye-bye."

Your baby tugs at a leaf on a house plant. "No," you say with a lower voice than "Bye-bye" and a different hand motion—probably a finger shaking or a sharp clap. Your child reacts to the serious tone of your voice and stops tugging at the leaf. Spanking is not necessary. Language, used effectively, is enough.

When you put out your arms in welcome and say, "Come here," your baby reacts with pleasure and reaches toward you. Your baby may not talk yet, but he or she is beginning to understand. These fledgling understandings make your baby a better companion, you a happier parent, and allow the relationship between the two of you to deepen.

Approximate age range: 9 to 12 months

BYE-BYE BLUES

The words "Bye-bye" can be very emotional to your child, and also to you when you are separating from your child–especially to go off to work or on a business trip that will keep you away from home for a while.

If you know that your child will be given good nurturing and responsible child care by your wife or another child care provider in your absence, you do not need to worry. Whatever anxiety you feel in leaving is best kept to yourself and not conveyed to your child. Children pick up their parents' tension and get unnecessarily upset by it. Babies cannot understand long explanations from grown-ups about where they are going, what they are going to do, and when they'll be back.

As a result, most parents find it easiest on all concerned to make their bye-byes short and sweet. Special rituals help everyone: breakfast together, a kiss on each cheek, a cheerful "Bye-bye" wave, and then leave. Once you've closed the door behind you, don't go back, even if you hear your baby crying. Doing so will only teach your baby to cry the next time. Is leaving cruel? Only if you leave your child with an incompetent caregiver. If that's the problem, deal with it directly.

If you leave your child in good hands, your cheerful leave-taking will encourage your baby to trust both you and the caregiver. This is not to say that your anxiety is wrong. On the contrary, it's perfectly natural, and other parents feel the same way. But don't make your baby suffer for your understandable nervousness.

As one father says, "At first you feel like a criminal. Then you get over it."

Approximate age range: 9 to 12 months

"Pat-a-Cake"

Speech-gesture games are winners now because they are fun and wonderfully educational. When you play the age-old game of "Pat-a-Cake" with your child, you are not only a barrel of fun, but you are acting as your child's first teacher, too. You are teaching your child to clap to rhythm, listen to rhyme, and to anticipate what's coming next. Your baby can't clap very well the first time around, but the more you play the game and the more fun you have, the more skilled your baby will become at this classic game.

How to play "Pat-a-Cake."

What you say	What you do
Pat-a-cake, pat-a-cake,	clap
Baker's man,	clap
Bake me a cake,	clap
As fast as you can;	clap
Roll it, stretch it,	pretend to do this
Mark it with a B,	write B on hand
So you can have cake	clap
With Baby and me!	clap

Suggested finger-play books.

PAT-A-CAKE and Other Play Rhymes by Joanna Cole and Stephanie Calmenson and *Hand Rhymes, Finger Rhymes,* and *Play Rhymes,* three books by Marc Brown, show how to play more speech-gesture games. These books will continue to entertain you and your child throughout the preschool years.

Performing "Pat-a-Cake" for others.

The more encouragement you give to your child attempting to play "Pat-a-Cake," the more your baby will want to develop the requisite skills. You may understandably want your baby to show off such skills for grandparents and friends. Just remember that performing for others is great fun for your baby, but there are times when Baby is shy or reluctant to do what you've asked. When this happens, there's not much you can do. Wait a while, and try again. No doubt, Grandma will still be there.

Approximate age range: 9 to 12 months

What Does "Developmentally Appropriate" Mean?

"Pat-a-Cake" is popular because the action involves listening skills and hand skills that babies at this stage are gaining with great personal satisfaction. In other words, it is developmentally appropriate. "Developmentally appropriate" means that an activity suits, or is appropriate for, the abilities of a child. The activity is neither too easy nor too hard. The ability to select developmentally appropriate activities for your child is one of the best skills you, as a parent, can learn. How do you learn it? By observing what your child can do and finding activities that suit those skills and that offer transitions to the next level of skills.

Approximate age range: 9 to 12 months

MORE ABOUT STRANGER ANXIETY

Fear of strangers (see page 133) peaks around nine to ten months, though not all babies have it. Babies who have received nurturing care from *several* familiar people—mother, father, siblings, grandparents, and perhaps a long-time baby-sitter as well—seem to be less likely to fear strangers than babies raised by one loving primary caretaker.

Parental leave problems.

Parents who have been home on parental leave may find it hard to go back to work at this time, particularly if their baby is experiencing fear of strangers. Parents can cope with this situation by creating an interim period during which one parent and a caregiver take care of the baby together. This period, which might last a weekend, several evenings, or a week, gives the baby a chance to get used to the new person. Establish an atmosphere of trust during the interim period, conveying enthusiasm for the caregiver and calmly leaving the baby alone with the caregiver for short periods. If the caregiver is warm and capable, you can trust that she will be able to soothe your baby and that your baby will get used to her—and even grow to trust and love her.

Why babies sometimes fear their daddies.

If you work long hours, your baby may perceive you as somewhat of a stranger and cling to your wife instead of going to you. It is generally a mistake to interpret a baby's preference for the mother at this age as a sign of either her superior parenting skills or your inferior ones. It may be wiser to conclude that the reason baby clings to Mommy is that you aren't around enough.

To alleviate this situation, consider ways to arrange time to be with your baby more, perhaps rising a little earlier in the morning to get your baby up so you can enjoy breakfast together. If you have to be away on business trips, antici-pate the possibility of your baby's fearfulness upon your return. Understand-ing your baby's fear will help you avoid getting hurt by it and help you feel more positive about making up lost time with your baby so that your relation-ship can be restored.

Approximate age range: 9 to 12 months

MAKING DATES AND GETTING BABY-SITTERS

It's important for you and your wife to get away from your children periodically so that you can rediscover the outside world together and your own adult relationship within it. The two of you may find it hard to leave your baby behind, but going out refreshes you and is good for everyone. The best baby-sitter is, of course, someone your baby is already familiar with—and someone you know and trust. Grandparents, aunts, and uncles are prime candidates, but unfortunately not every family has them living close by. Don't wait until the last minute to look for baby-sitters. Help your wife keep a list of good possibilities, and don't assume that it's the mother's job to make all the arrangements. A very nice treat for your wife would be an invitation for an old-fashioned date that comes with a special new-fashion feature: a great baby-sitter already contracted for.

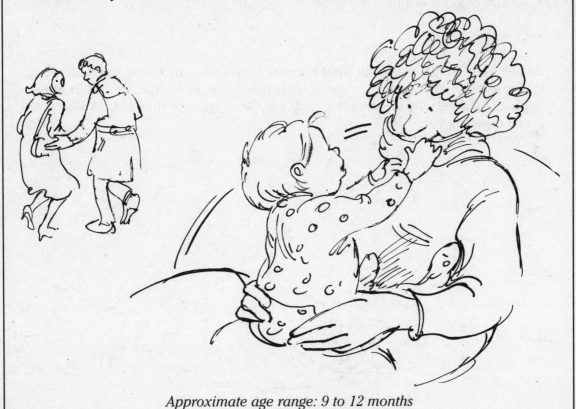

Approximate age range: 9 to 12 months

THE PLEASURE OF PLAYING ALONE

While babies this age love to play with people, they are also content to play by themselves for short periods of time. Indeed, it is good for babies to play alone—going according to their own whims and at their own pace. While your baby is playing alone, you should be near enough to supervise.

How long will Baby play alone?

Babies' fascination with their hands, feet, and objects keeps them occupied until they become bored. When this happens, they will let you know! Just as you respect your baby's need to enjoy private time, you need also to respect your baby's need to tell you when it's over.

Where babies can play alone.

- A baby exploratorium. (See opposite page.)

- Crib or playpen.

Babies seem to like to play in their cribs or playpens if they have interesting things to play with and if they are in fairly quiet moods, such as before or after naptime. Babies who are crawling may want "out" sooner than babies who aren't crawling yet.

Approximate age range: 9 to 12 months

BABY EXPLORATORIUM

A baby exploratorium is a special place you create in your home for your baby to explore without restrictions. This place is not only baby-proof in an up-to-date manner (see page 161), but it is also a hands-on baby museum. Everything in the baby exploratorium is meant to be explored by the baby. You can turn an entire room into a baby exploratorium, or block off part of a large room, with hassocks and stuffed chairs. Use one of the stuffed chairs to sit in and rest—until needed. If your baby is happily and safely occupied, you might be able to chat on the phone or flip through a magazine. Note: a baby exploratorium is a nice, safe place for your baby to entertain a guest of the same age. Babies this age like to watch each other play.

Interesting, safe objects to put in the baby exploratorium.

- Responsive toys that do something as a result of baby's action. A jack-in-the-box is a good example—keep in mind that babies can only make a very simple one pop up.

- Simple toys that babies can take apart and put back together

- Baby toys of varying shapes, weights, and textures

- Toys that make noise, such as rattles

- Small blocks

- Balls to roll

- Things to bang together

- Things to push and poke

- An unbreakable baby mirror

- Baby books

- Teddy bear

Approximate age range: 9 to 12 months

PEEK-A-BOO

We have seen that as babies grow, they observe objects and learn the names for them. Another aspect of their learning continues to involve the concept of object permanence. (See also page 93.) If an object is removed from sight, does it still exist? Some of Baby's favorite games are disappearance games that explore this question.

Peek-a-boo.

There is a reason why peek-a-boo is so fascinating for babies. If Daddy hides his face behind a pillow, is Daddy still there? The doubt in a baby's mind is what makes the rediscovery of Daddy a thrill over and over again until one day when your child is older, you'll realize that you haven't been playing peek-a-boo for a while. Though your child may still enjoy playing it, it is no longer an essential part of your child's self-motivated curriculum. Your child has already mastered the concept. Yes, Daddy is still there.

Lose it, find it.

This activity is a sophisticated version of peek-a-boo. Babies invent it themselves; they have in their hands something that they deliberately lose. They might drop it in a hole or throw it from their crib or high chair. Then they look to see where it is and then work to get it back. If they can get it back themselves, they are greatly satisfied and will proceed to repeat the game unless it no longer interests them.

Toys on a leash.

If you haven't done this before, leash a few toys to the high chair so that your child can throw them off and reel them in. After watching parents reel in the toys enthusiastically a few times, babies want to try it themselves. A few cautions: don't make the leash so long that the object lands on the floor and gets dirty. Don't leash toys to a crib or playpen in which babies could choke on the cord. Last, don't leash a bottle to a high chair. If your baby throws a bottle, simply remove it and provide a toy instead. Your actions will convey that food is not a toy. Babies who throw their bottles away are probably not hungry.

Approximate age range: 9 to 12 months

Simple Mailbox Toys

Babies this age may like mailbox toys and boxes with one or more holes in them through which objects can be dropped or "mailed." You can make such a toy by cutting a hole in a cardboard box. The hole doesn't need to be a particular shape. Start with a big hole that will accommodate a number of small toys. Use a box that your child will be able to lift by him- or herself to retrieve what's underneath.

One father's rainy day, last-resort inspiration.

"The best toy I ever made for my twins was simply a cardboard box turned upside down. I cut a big slot in it and gave my babies margarine tub lids. Why? Because I couldn't think of anything else. They loved dropping the lids through the slot until they were out of lids. Then, we lifted up the box and found all the lids underneath. They were thrilled. This toy kept them busy for at least an hour."

Approximate age range: 9 to 12 months

Baby's First Birthday

It may seem impossible that your baby is now one year old. So much has happened in a year! Since your one-year-old doesn't understand what birthdays and birthday parties are, you can choose between two basic ways to celebrate: one, to have a grown-up party at which you and your wife celebrate; or, two, to have a real kids' birthday party at which you provide your child with birthday party customs on an age-appropriate level. You can also combine the two, but watch out that things don't get too confusing. Confusion is not what you need. Congratulations!

Approximate age range: 9 to 12 months

HOW TO GIVE A REAL KID'S BIRTHDAY PARTY FOR A ONE-YEAR-OLD

1. Invite one to four children accompanied by a parent or baby-sitter, explaining when the party starts and ends. One hour is max. Ask the parents to bring the children's bottles and cups.

2. As you help your child open presents, let all the kids play with the wrapping paper, ribbons, cards, and the presents, if appropriate. Have some of your child's toys about for children also to play with during this time.

3. When the time seems right, serve party food to the children at a low table, or have them sit on grown-ups' laps at a regular table. A good menu is unfrosted cupcakes or muffins (frosted ones are too messy, though fun for photos) and juice. At this age, a fancy birthday paper tablecloth and matching napkins will go unappreciated. Put a candle on the birthday child's cupcake and help him or her blow it out. Sing "Happy Birthday," and serve milk or juice. Ask a friend to serve the grown-ups. (This is also a good job for a helpful grandparent.)

4. Ask another friend to take photos. (This is a good job for another helpful grandparent, should you be so lucky.)

5. While the kids are at the table, try playing "Pat-a-Cake" together. Parents will probably want to help.

6. Let the children down to play. Don't try to organize games, and don't whoop things up. Stay calm and don't be surprised if children cry for perfectly normal reasons.

7. When the party is over, give each child a new rattle or squeak toy as a party favor.

Approximate age range: 9 to 12 months

CHAPTER FIVE:
12 TO 18 MONTHS

The natural curiosity of babies motivates them to learn. They don't learn the way you do—by reading books, watching TV, and attending lectures. There is no middleman for babies. They learn by firsthand experience. They learn by touching and exploring things themselves.

Curious babies are nomadic. Crawling, cruising, or walking, they stop in one place only to explore what's there. When they are finished exploring, they move on. To teach children this age, you have to be willing to safeguard them as they explore the world. You need to respect their curiosity, allow them independence (as long as they are safe), and supply language to enhance the their experience. It's not easy! But the more you understand how important this stage is, the better you'll be able to cope with it.

Approximate age range: 12 to 18 months

Control freaks beware.

Caring for a children between twelve and eighteen months of age can be a frustrating job, especially for people who like to manage other people's actions. You make things tough on yourself when you try to make a curious, exploring baby do what *you* want, rather than what he or she wants. If you let your child lead the way and realize all you have to do is talk about things and prevent disasters, you'll have an easier time. After a while, you might even find that it's interesting to let go of your adult mind and see the world from a baby's point of view.

Approximate age range: 12 to 18 months

DRINKING FROM A CUP

Babies are still practicing how to hold a cup with both hands, lift it, and drink from it. They're getting better at this, but still—you have to expect spills. Some babies will not forsake their bottles. If your baby is a bottle lover, don't worry about it. Casually, offer the cup from time to time. One of these days, your baby will be interested. If Baby is still breast-feeding and both Baby and Mother are happy with the arrangement, don't worry about that either. Breast, bottle, cup: all are perfectly fine ways for your baby to drink liquids, which is, after all, the point.

Approximate age range: 12 to 18 months

EATING WITH A SPOON

Babies learn by imitating. They observe you and others eat with knives, forks, and spoons; and they watch you feed them with a spoon. Sooner or later, they reach out and grab the spoon. They want to see if they can feed themselves.

The desire to feed oneself with a spoon is a developmental milestone! But desire alone does not signify success. Your child is only a beginner. As with other milestones, your positive, patient reaction to your child's ambitions will help to determine whether or not your child develops self-confidence. So be patient.

At first, let your baby help you hold the spoon. When you think your baby can use the spoon alone, put something sticky on the spoon like mashed potatoes. Save peas and carrots for later.

Siblings may laugh at babies who feed themselves with a great mess. You can encourage such siblings to be more helpful by showing them how to wipe the baby's face with a warm, damp washcloth. They can also amuse Baby by letting Baby try to feed them!

Approximate age range: 12 to 18 months

SLEEPING & WAKING

Young children need plenty of sleep, and routine bedtimes help them and you make sure they get it. Some children in this age range no longer need two naps a day. If your child drops a nap, make sure he or she still has a quiet rest period for about an hour each day.

Cranky wakers.

Some children wake up pleasantly in the morning; others wake up cranky. The cranky ones usually are hard-to-waken children; they are cranky because you have had to wake them up for one reason or another. If you have to wake up a hard-to-waken child, experiment with various wake-up routines in order to find the one that works best. You might try waking your child and playing a tape of children's songs for fifteen minutes before getting him or her out of the crib. Some parents who take their children to a baby-sitter or day care don't wake them at all. They just scoop them out of bed and take them as they are. For this to work, you need a willing child care provider with a supply (that you provide) of clothes, diapers, and breakfast foods.

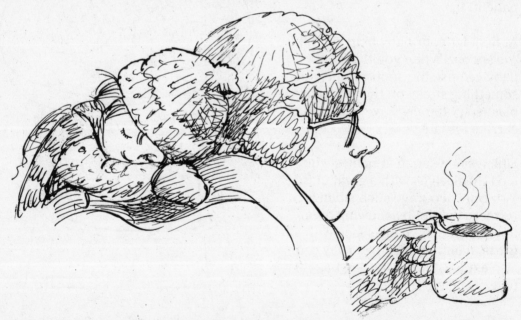

Safety note: always hold hot drinks so that they cannot spill on your child.

Approximate age range: 12 to 18 months

NAPTIME RITUALS

One or two naps continue to help young children progress happily through their days. As your child grows, however, you have to adapt your nap rituals to his or her new understandings. Some nap rituals that may work now are:

1. One or two* naptime books

2. One or two* naptime lullabies

3. A naptime lullaby tape played softly in a tape recorder

4. A teddy bear or doll or special blanket** to hold, and/or

5. A calm and pleasant discussion about what activities will take place when naptime is over.

* It's best to stick with a set number of books or songs so that you avoid getting into the "one more" rut.

** Special objects are great, but try not to encourage your child to become dependent on them. One way to avoid object dependency is to let your child select a different cuddly object each naptime. This way, when your child is at Grandma's, he or she won't have a fit if the teddy bear was left home.

Approximate age range: 12 to 18 months

TOILETING AWARENESS

At this age babies may begin to tell you in words or motions when their diapers need to be changed. When this happens, your reaction is important. It's wise to react calmly. You help your child develop a positive self-image by treating bodily functions in an accepting, matter-of-fact manner. Scorn and disgust on your part teaches your child that there is something wrong with what he or she is telling you.

Approximate age range: 12 to 18 months

LEARNING THROUGH OBSERVATION

Your baby may see other children sitting on a potty seat and be curious about the experience. Explain that this is where big boys and girls go pee and poo (use whatever terms you are comfortable with). Your child may want to try sitting on a potty seat. Since babies this age can sit still for a while, they can actually do this. You may want to buy a potty seat for this purpose, but don't pressure your child into toilet training. Just introduce the concept for now, and realize that one of the main ways children learn is through imitation.

Approximate age range: 12 to 18 months

BATH TIME

Bath time and water play continue to hold the potential for great fun. So, if possible, don't rush these events. Make them an event that happens on your watch, and let your child enjoy them to the fullest—during the bath and afterward, wrapped in a towel in your arms. Continue to develop bath rituals that are mutually satisfying to the two of you.

Approximate age range: 12 to 18 months

WATER PLAY

Instead of a bath, let your baby play in a baby pool outside (if the weather is suitable). But put only an inch or two of water in the pool and stay close by—really close by. Babies this age like to try to stand up in a pool, and they can easily slip. Put some bath toys in the pool and let your baby play as long as he or she likes without getting chilled. At the end, if you like, try shampooing your child's hair. If this seems like more trouble than it's worth, skip it.

Approximate age range: 12 to 18 months

DRESSING...

In one sense, babies now are easier to dress. They are more apt, for example, to push their hands and feet into the arms and legs of their clothing. Respond with enthusiasm, expressing your thanks, and perhaps even suggesting other ways to help.

In another sense, though, as babies become fascinated with buttons, zippers, and socks, they can impede the dressing process. You might give your child a sock to play with while you are putting on another sock.

Clothing toys.

Clothing toys are fun for children now. A teddy bear with a zipper jacket can a distraction for a baby being dressed. Baby books with zippers, snaps, buttons, and ties are good to read together.

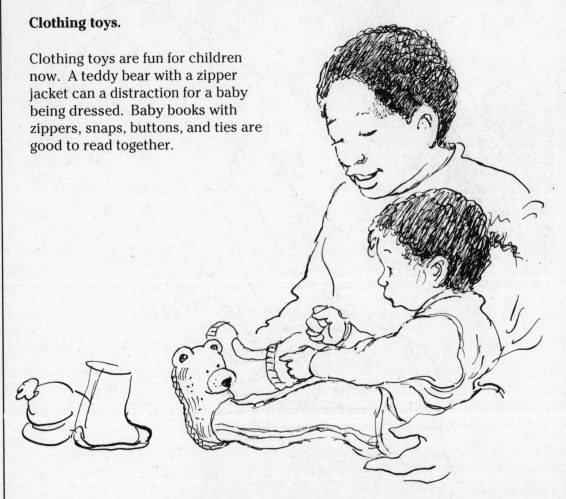

Approximate age range: 12 to 18 months

...And Undressing

There are two reasons why your baby may like to take clothing off: one, because it's uncomfortable, and two, because it's fun. The former reason may apply to a diaper that's too full to wear. The latter may apply to socks. Socks are an interesting challenge. You reach forward, grab hold, pull—and off they come! If diapers are a problem, change them more often and fasten them more snugly. If socks are a problem, cover them with shoes that your baby can't pull off. Or, treat socks like a toy. *You pull them off, and I'll put them on.*

Approximate age range: 12 to 18 months

ARE YOU BORED WITH BABY?

While your baby may find the fringe on the bottom of the couch fascinating for ten minutes, you may find it fascinating for only one. So you say, "Come on, look at this," pointing to a new toy truck, but Baby is still fluttering the fringe. You sigh. Never in your life has time passed more slowly. What can you do when you find yourself in this numbed state? Happily, a number of things:

• Suggest an alternate tried-and-true activity that you know your baby loves and that you like too, such as having a bath.

• Place your baby in a "baby exploratorium" (see page 177), where you can safely read a magazine and keep an eye on him or her at the same time.

• Take your baby on an errand you need to accomplish. Babies in backpacks and car seats are usually content to observe the world around them or fall asleep.

What *not* to do when you're bored by babies.

• Don't force babies to explore things more quickly than they want.

• Don't make them play a game that they don't want to play but you do.

• Don't blame the baby for boring you. The baby is content; you're the grumpy one.

• Don't leave babies alone. Babies this age cannot be trusted to be safe. They can pull books down upon themselves, knock over lamps, touch hot things, rip up letters, and fall down stairs. They always need to be watched.

Approximate age range: 12 to 18 months

IS BABY BORED WITH YOU?

Babies get bored when forced to stay in the same place or play with the same toy for too long. The reason babies like to move about as they explore is that they can change the object of their curiosity as often as necessary. Playpens, cribs, and car seats can be fascinating places for a while, but sooner or later they become dull, and babies want to escape from them.

Babies can also get bored with adults who talk too little or too much. Babies like adults who talk pleasantly about what babies are doing. But adults can overdo this role, yakking incessantly into a baby's ear about *everything* the baby is doing. After a while, babies may tune the noise out.

If you want to be interesting to your child, be interested in what your child is doing. But don't overdo it. If you overdo it, you can smother your child and prevent your child from discovering the thrill of learning on his or her own. Children who have been overstimulated by their parents may rely on them for experiences. Such a child at day care may seem to be bored, when the truth could be that what the child lacks is a sense of curiosity and self-motivation.

Babies won't get bored if you give them developmentally appropriate experiences (see page 173) that you allow to them to enjoy and that you reflect, but not smother, with language.

Approximate age range: 12 to 18 months

CLAPPING AND BANGING

Babies continue to practice clapping their hands. Sometimes they'll initiate the activity themselves when they hear music. They love to have you join in.

Clapping to music.

You can always find songs on the radio for you and your baby to clap to. You might also want to buy some tapes or CDs of music that is specifically geared to very young children.

Clapping games and songs.

Babies still like to play "Pat-a-Cake." (See page 172.) Instead of finding this game boring, your increasingly skillful baby finds it more and more satisfying.

Clapping instruments.

Babies like to hold things in their hands and clap them together—in effect, creating their own percussion instruments. They might do this with little toys, small blocks, or plastic container lids. If you like, you can pick up two blocks and join your baby's rhythm section.

Banging on homemade drums.

Turn a wooden salad bowl upside down, and you have a homemade drum. Hand your baby a wooden spoon for a drumstick, and then cover your ears.

Approximate age range: 12 to 18 months

TOY WORKBENCH

It's not just noise that babies like to make. What they really like is to bang something and see what happens. They like to observe the results of their actions. Noise doesn't have to be the only result.

Workbench-type toys.

A workbench-type toy enables a child to bang a hammer wholeheartedly against pegs. The banging has two intriguing results: noise and the movement of the pegs. When the pegs are pounded through, the bench can be turned over with pegs awaiting.

This toy may or may not interest your child right away. You may have to wait a month or two. For now, demonstrate how to bang the pegs, turning the mallet over to your child as soon as he or she expresses an interest in using it. If your baby can use the hammer and wants to, stay close by to make sure the mallet is used safely.

If your child does not yet have the strength or interest to pound the pegs through, let matters be for a while. In time, your child will be able to pound the pegs and be interested in doing so. Unless your child can do the job alone, he or she will probably not be interested in your ability to do it—so don't bother showing off.

Approximate age range: 12 to 18 months

Ringing Bells

A bell is a perfect first instrument for a child because it is so easy to hold and play. All your baby has to do is move it. You can buy small bells in toy stores and musical instrument stores. Buy two so you and your baby can ring bells together. Because bells may not be nontoxic and because they can be noisy, you may want to keep the bells in a special place and only bring them out for special musical jam sessions.

CLUSTER BELLS

TEA BELL

WRIST BELLS

Approximate age range: 12 to 18 months

DIGGING IN SAND WITH SHOVELS

As soon as children can dig with a scoop or shovel, they are ready for the sandbox. Children like to play with sand because it is a flexible material that they can manipulate and change. To make a sandbox, pour a few inches of sand into a small wading pool. Add a few small shovels, pails, plastic containers, and maybe even a dump truck. Stay close by to supervise. From the beginning, teach your child not to eat or throw sand. Explain why in short, clear sentences, such as: "We don't eat sand because it can make us sick," and "We don't throw sand because it can hurt other children." If your child cannot obey these rules, simply remove him or her from the sandbox. Don't make a big deal of it. It may take a little while for your child to learn the etiquette of sandbox play.

Approximate age range: 12 to 18 months

PUTTING THINGS IN HOLES

More complex mailbox toys and shape boxes.

Because children still like to put things in holes and are getting better at it, they may be ready for more complex mailboxes and shape boxes. To use these toys, children must fit three-dimensional shapes into holes of the same size. Many children are given these toys before they are able to use them correctly. If this is the case with your baby, just wait a while. Bring it out occasionally, demonstrating how to use it without pressuring your baby to do the same independently. You might want to try guiding your child's hand to the right holes. Your baby might prefer to play with the shapes in other ways, and that's fine, too. In fact, it's creative!

Watch the nose and ears.

Marbles, pretzels, crayon pieces, buttons, tiny toys, peas and carrots—doctors have retrieved all of these objects from babies' noses and ears. So, in addition to watching what babies put in their mouths, watch what they put in their other orifices, too.

The picking up game.

Putting toys away can become a game if the object is to drop them in boxes or put them in the correct places. If you're clever, you can make work fun, especially if you join in. When your child is this age, you'll probably do most of the work yourself, but at the same time, you'll be instilling in your child a valuable concept—putting toys away when you're through with them.

Approximate age range: 12 to 18 months

INVENTING GAMES WITH JUNK MATERIALS

Once you grasp the concept of what is developmentally appropriate (see page 173), you'll be able to invent games for your baby, using junk materials, such as paper towel rolls and plastic margarine containers. Junk materials are great because they cost nothing and inspire some of the best games. Your enthusiasm for a game of your own invention will make your "junk" toy more exciting to your child than most purchased toys. The trick to making up successful games for babies is to stay simple, focus on your child's present abilities, and let your imagination go. Be inventive; and, if so inspired, be a little silly.

Talking through tubes.

Put a paper towel roll up to your mouth and talk or sing through it, holding the other end of the tube gently against your child's ear. Let your child talk through it too, holding the tube against your ear.

Junk mail game.

Turn a cardboard box upside down and cut a big slot in it to make a mailbox. Then, let your child "mail" your junk mail in the slot.

Paper towel roll game.

Drop things down a paper towel roll and see where they come out. It's just that simple—and fun!

GO!

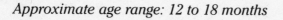

Approximate age range: 12 to 18 months

SMALL BLOCK PLAY

Small blocks, 1-2" square, are a great toy for babies this age because they are too big to be swallowed but small enough to be handled easily. Larger building blocks are too heavy for children this age. Small blocks are usually plastic, plain wood, or wood painted with nontoxic paint.

Rows and columns.

It's interesting to observe what children do with small blocks. Between the ages of six and twelve months, they may hold a block in each hand and then put the two blocks together in a line. Between twelve and eighteen months, they may try to place one block on top of another to make a little tower.

What you can do.

Observe your child carefully. If your child is making a line or a tower, make one like it yourself. Be a copycat. Talk about what you are both doing. "One block here and one block here." If you think your child is ready for it, advance the challenge slightly. "I'm going to add another block to my line," or "I'm going to put another block on top of my tower." You can even count your blocks aloud, not to teach your child to count necessarily but rather to get across the concept of counting. Counting aloud as you play together provides your child with a sense of numbers to be developed in future years.

Approximate age range: 12 to 18 months

PARALLEL PLAY

Children at this age don't really play together; instead they play by themselves near each other. In other words, they play parallel to each other rather than with each other. In this way, they enjoy being together, often stopping to observe each other thoughtfully.

Sharing toys.

Sometimes what one child is doing with a toy will fascinate another child so much that the latter will try to take the toy away. When this kind of trouble erupts, try to avoid overreacting. Realize that the essence of the problem is that both children want to play with a fascinating toy, which is why, often, all you have to do to calm the situation down is distract one or the other child with another equally exciting toy or activity. If you want to say something, you might say, "We want everyone to have a toy to play with."

Approximate age range: 12 to 18 months

SCRIBBLING, DRAWING, OR WRITING?

Babies like to make marks on paper with crayons, an activity commonly called "scribbling." But what is it, exactly, that babies are trying to do? At first, they may just be experimenting with moving and banging a crayon against paper to see the results of their actions. As they get older, they may be trying to draw a picture; or, having seen you write, they may be trying to write. It's also possible that they may be doing each of these things at different times or even all three at the same time on one piece of paper. You never know for sure, and it doesn't really matter because all three activities are worthwhile.

To encourage these activities, keep paper and fat crayons on hand. Envelopes that come in the mail, particularly large white envelopes, are a free source of sturdy paper. Fat crayons are preferable to thin ones because they are easier to hold, less breakable, and less likely to be inserted into noses and ears. You can usually buy fat crayons wherever regular-size crayons are sold. Make sure they are nontoxic. Most likely, your child will hold them in his or her fist.

Expect a little mess.

Babies don't understand why it's okay to draw on paper and not on the table. Even if they did understand, they might not be able to keep their marks on the paper only. You can help to prevent messes by giving your child big pieces of paper to draw on or by covering the entire surface with paper. Taping paper down with masking tape will hold it firmly in place.

BECCA at 14 mos.

Approximate age range: 12 to 18 months

CLAY & PLAY DOUGH

Clay and play dough are excellent art materials for one-and-a-half-year-olds because clay and play dough are easy to manipulate, thus allowing children freedom of expression. Children can pound clay noisily or quietly tear it into tiny bits. Make sure the clay and play dough you give your child is nontoxic. For young children, the advantage of play dough over clay is that it is usually softer.

Picking up clay and play dough.

Herein lies the disadvantage of these otherwise swell play materials. Little sticky bits can drop to the floor, attach themselves to the bottoms of your shoes, and be trampled around your home. Anticipate the problem ahead of time. Either spread newspaper on the floor to catch the falling bits or end the activity when it starts to go downhill, so to speak. Store clay and play dough in covered containers so they don't dry out.

Supervise closely.

Babies like to put little balls of clay and play dough in their ears and noses. They also like to eat these materials. So watch carefully. The best way to do this is to play *with* your child during the activity.

Play dough recipe.

Mix:
2 cups flour
3/4 cup salt
1/2 cup water
1 tablespoon salad oil

Work with your hands until dough is smooth. Store in a plastic bag in the refrigerator.

Approximate age range: 12 to 18 months

PLAY BALL!

Your baby is probably ready to play a little ball now. Think of all the skills that have led up to this! Over the last year your baby learned how to hold on to something, then how to let go of it, and then actually how to throw it. Playing ball is a perfect activity for children this age because it not only enables children to exercise their arm muscles but also promotes a wonderful kind of give-and-take social interaction with others, especially you.

THE RED SOX ARE COUNTING ON YOU JOANNE!

Keep it simple.

Your child is not yet ready for the major leagues. Make sure that your initial ball games (see opposite page) are simple and enjoyable. Don't always pressure your child to do better. Accept your child's abilities as they are.

Approximate age range: 12 to 18 months

BABY'S FIRST BALL GAMES

Small balls.

Think of yourself as a ball machine. You provide the balls, and the baby throws them. You collect them and give them back to Baby. It's interesting to note that some babies throw sidearm and others throw overhand. Still others practice both ways. This activity is best played outside.

Rolling big balls back and forth.

Sit opposite your child. Both of you spread your legs out so they touch and make a barrier that prevents the ball from rolling away. Take turns rolling the ball back and forth. Too simple? Maybe for you, but not for your child. This kind of back and forth activity is great for kids this age.

Beanbag toss.

Toss beanbags into a big, open cardboard box. Couldn't be simpler and couldn't be more fun. Try this when your child has friends over. Have your child and playmates stand close enough to score most of the time. At this age everyone should be a winner. If you don't have any beanbags, fill Ziploc bags with beans, or get older siblings to sew beanbags for presents.

Approximate age range: 12 to 18 months

BECOMING AN UPRIGHT PERSON

Creeping and crawling are fun, but babies naturally want to progress to the next achievable challenge—standing and walking. Most children learn to walk between twelve and fourteen months of age. By the time they are eighteen months old, they can walk well without any help. But this achievement doesn't happen overnight; it's the result of a gradual process, each stage of which you can assist by understanding and accepting where your baby is and being ready to help him or her reach the next stage. Below is a list of some of the milestones babies go through as they learn to stand up and walk on their own. Your baby may have accomplished some of them already.

Upright person milestones.

1. Pull oneself up

2. Stand holding on

3. Lower oneself back down

4. Stand alone

5. Go from sitting to standing alone

6. Go from stooping to standing alone

7. Cruise about, holding on to things

8. Take a walk holding on to you

It's time for a household safety check.

Ask yourself: what places can your newly upright baby get to now? Make sure that everything your baby can reach now is safe to touch. Keep close watch.

Approximate age range: 12 to 18 months

CRUISING & WALKING

Your child's life greatly expands with walking; the whole world opens up and becomes ever more interesting. Realizing this, you need to adapt your role. Your new job is to guard a cruising nomad. To do this job well, you have to be very patient because what may be fascinating to your nomadic child may be boring to you. Unless the place you are in is baby-proof, you have to walk slowly and observantly around with your child. When the phone rings, you can't just leave. You have to take your baby with you or put your child in a playpen or crib. Babies are safe there—as long as they can't climb out.

Where to visit with a baby nomad.

Try to visit homes that are baby-proof. In hazardous homes, be prepared to deal with a frustrated baby who doesn't want to be restrained in your arms. Having some toys along will help. Instead of visiting friends whose homes are not baby-proof, invite them to your home and chat with them in a room where your baby can roam.

Walking up and down stairs.

Just as stairs presented a challenge to your crawling baby so do they now to your walking baby. Devote a few minutes each day to stair practice. It's one of the most boring jobs of parenthood, but it doesn't have to last forever. Put gates at the tops and bottoms of stairways, and close them when you can't stand to do stair duty any longer.

Falling down and getting hurt.

As children learn to walk, they inevitably fall down and get hurt. Mishaps can be painful for your child—and for you, too! But as one father says, "I have observed two phenomena in this regard: one, that when our son learned what it was to fall, he also learned to hug and cuddle. Before that, he had never been much for snuggling, but with his new freedom and accompanying difficulties, he learned one of the main values of other people—they comfort you when you're down. Second, I discovered that what other parents advised us was indeed true—a child reacts much the way his parents react to his falls. If they make a big fuss, the child makes a big fuss. If they don't overreact, the child learns to take the bumps in stride."

Approximate age range: 12 to 18 months

Music & Dance

Babies this age continue to enjoy music and dancing. The more activities you can offer in this regard, the happier they'll be. And you don't have to be an opera star or a tap dancer either. Babies are not fussy. Whatever level your skills are on is okay with your baby, as long as you put your heart into it. All you need is a little spontaneity.

Three ways to dance with a baby.

1. Hold your baby in your arms and step to the music.
2. Bounce your baby on your lap to music.
3. Hold your baby's hands, and follow your baby's lead on the kitchen dance floor.

Songs babies like.

Babies like whatever you like. If you want to sing your alma mater, go right ahead. If you want to sing the top ten songs from your high school days, your most welcome audience probably will be your baby.

What if you don't know any traditional songs for children?

Go into a tape store and buy a tape featuring traditional songs for very young children. There are lots of them. Play the tape in the car when you are traveling with your child. In time you'll know it by heart and will be able to sing along. Your baby may be able to sing parts of it, too.

Approximate age range: 12 to 18 months

FINGER PLAY SONGS

Finger play songs are ones you can act out with your hands and fingers. Sometimes they are called "speech-gesture games." (See page 172.) "Itsy Bitsy Spider"* is a prime example. If you don't remember the hand motions, ask an older child or early childhood teacher to teach them to you.

"Itsy Bitsy Spider"

Itsy Bitsy Spider
Went up the waterspout,
Down came the rain
And washed the spider out.
Out came the sun
And dried up all the rain,
And the Itsy Bitsy Spider
Went up the spout again.

*Also called "Eentsy Weentsy Spider."

What can your child teach YOU?

Children who go to day care may try to teach you finger play songs. If you don't understand what your baby is doing, discreetly ask the teacher to demonstrate.

Grandparents as audience.

Finger plays are great for showing off to grandparents. If your baby is shy, perform them as a duet.

WHERE IS THUMBKIN?
(sung to the tune of Frère Jacques)

Approximate age range: 12 to 18 months

FIRST WORDS

It's interesting to note that most babies learn to both walk and talk between twelve and fourteen months of age. Perhaps Mother Nature realized that ambulatory babies might want and need to communicate. They might need to cry "Da-da" when they get into a jam, and they might need to say "Ba-ba" when they are hungry for a bottle.

At first, your baby may only say two or three words, but slowly this vocabulary will increase. Reward your child's language with delight, enriching the experience by repeating your baby's words, often in whole sentences. For example, if your baby says "Ca" for "Cat," you might say, "Yes, there's the cat."

As you play with and care for your baby every day, use language freely, naming familiar things, such as: teddy bear, block, rattle, sock, jersey, diaper, and calling familiar people by their names. Your baby is listening to you because what you say is stimulating.

Approximate age range: 12 to 18 months

"LOOK AT THAT!" GAME

To play this game (which doesn't seem like a game to anyone but a baby), all you do is point to something interesting and obvious and say, "Look at that! It's a fire truck!" Or just, "Look at the fire truck!" Your baby responds by looking at the object you've selected. That's all there is to it. You can play it anytime, on walks, at home, in the car, in the pediatrician's office. Don't overdo it, and don't play it when your baby's too tired to focus. What this game does is teach babies the names of things. Babies like it so much that someday you'll be surprised to hear your baby say to you, "Look at dat!"

Approximate age range: 12 to 18 months

ACTION RHYMES

Action rhymes, also called "speech-gesture games" (see page 172) are still immensely popular with this age group. Because they combine movement, rhythm, and language, they are educational, too. If you haven't taught your child to play "Pat-a-Cake" (see page 172) or "Itsy Bitsy Spider" (page 211) yet, it's time to do so. Following are some other action rhymes you and your child might enjoy.

(Action: bounce your child on your knee, "dropping" child at the end.)

Trot, trot to Boston,
Trot, trot to Town,
Trot, trot to Paris,
Where we all fall down

(Action: bounce your child
on your knees, changing
speed with the various
verses.)

This is the way the Daddy rides,
The Daddy rides,
The Daddy rides,
This is the way the Daddy rides,
All the way to town-o.

This is the way the Mommy rides,
The Mommy rides,
The Mommy rides,
This is the way the Mommy rides,
All the way to town-o.

This is the way the Baby rides,
The Baby rides,
The Baby rides,
This is the way the Baby rides,
All the way to town-o.

Approximate age range: 12 to 18 months

CREATING YOUR OWN ACTION RHYMES

If you have a sense of rhyme and rhythm, put it to use as you take care of your child. Make up sensible or silly poems, or even rap poems, to go with actions your baby can perform. If you discover that you have a talent for this, record your rhymes on a tape that your child can listen to without you.

(Action: wave to each of these things at bedtime.)

Bye-bye, cat,
Bye-bye, spoon,
Bye-bye, window,
Bye-bye, moon.

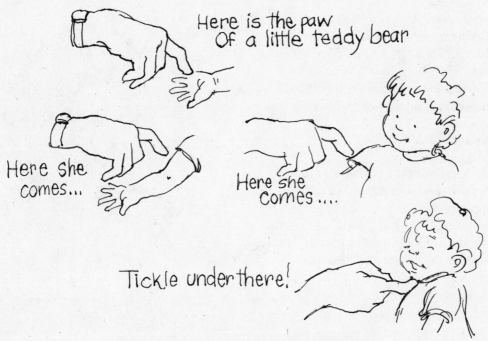

Approximate age range: 12 to 18 months

BABY RESPONDS TO REQUESTS

One of the best ways to teach your child to respond to your requests is through the following game, which you can easily play at the changing table.

May I please have it?

In this game you ask your child to give you whatever he or she has in hand. Name the object you want, for example: "May I please have the block?" If your child hands it to you, take it with great pleasure. Then give it back to your child, saying, "Now you have the block," or whatever seems natural. Keep the game going back and forth until your child (or you) loses interest. The ability to play this game shows that your child can understand language and respond to it.

Other times, when you are not playing the game, you may notice that your child has picked up something dirty or dangerous. Calmly say, "May I please have it?" It helps to have something else to give your child to replace what you took away.

Listen attentively. Some day your child may say something to you like "Have it?" which means "May I please have it?" in baby talk. Your child is making a sentencelike request to you! This is a language milestone.

Other requests.

You may find that your baby is learning now to respond to other simple requests, such as "Come here" and "Put that down." Perhaps you can think up games to make these responses palatable, too.

Approximate age range: 12 to 18 months

BABY GIVES COMMANDS

"Gimme dat!"

Sometimes your baby points to something and says, "Dat!" or "Gimme dat!" What should you do? If possible, give it to your child. You may be able to get your child to say, "Dat, Peez," which means "That, please," by always saying the phrase the polite way and hoping your child will imitate you.

If you don't want to give the child a particular object (because it's breakable or otherwise dangerous), just say simply and firmly, "No, that's not for babies." Then turn away from the coveted object and distract your child with something else exciting, naming it as you hand it to your child.

Mothers vs. fathers re "Gimme dat."

What one parent says a child can't have, another parent or baby-sitter may say a child can have. Thus, two adults may feel pitted against each other. Who's right? And who gets to decide? The situation can be sticky. To cope, realize first of all that you both agree on the extremes. No, Baby cannot have a crystal glass to play with; and yes, Baby can have the teddy bear.

But what if Daddy says, "No, Baby can't have my spoon," and Mommy says, "But I give her *my* spoon all the time." Now you have a choice. You can either stick to your guns and not be bossed around, particularly in front of your child, who may learn to play one parent against another. Or upon reflection, you may realize that your wife has a point—your spoon probably is okay for Baby to use. In which case, you may wish to shrug and say something like "Really? Well then, okay, I'll give her mine too." From such an example, your baby may learn that the two of you can give and take, and that disagreement can be a constructive process. Children absorb these lessons at an early age.

On the other hand, incessant disagreement about what's appropriate for your baby to have and not have may drive everyone crazy. If this is the situation, sit down with your wife and talk things out. What you don't want to do is conclude that fathers just don't understand anything about babies!

Approximate age range: 12 to 18 months

CONVERSING WITH PEOPLE

Once babies learn a few words, they may incorporate them into their babbling language (see page 162). When you converse with your baby, your baby may talk right back to you with a mixture of babbling words and real words. If possible, record some of these conversations with a tape recorder or a video recorder. One day the tapes will bring back precious memories.

Approximate age range: 12 to 18 months

TALKING TO TOYS

Sometimes your baby will carry on conversations with his or her toys. When this is going on, enjoy the moment. Observe with wonder, but wait to intercede. Appreciate the fact that, for the moment, you are not necessary.

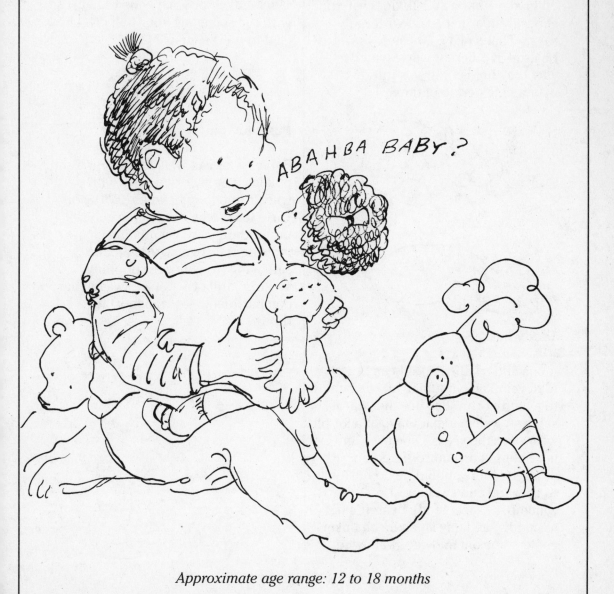

Approximate age range: 12 to 18 months

GREAT TOYS FOR...

Your child may already have some of these toys but not have been old enough to appreciate them. It's time to reintroduce them. Even still, your child may not be able to do what you expect him or her to do with the toys. That's okay. These toys can be used in different ways, which is why they hold children's interest over a long period of time.

Teddy bear.

A one-and-a-half-year-old can begin to develop an emotional attachment to a teddy bear. Be sure the bear is safe and well made; it may get a lot of wear over the years. The eyes and nose should be embroidered on securely; there should be no buttons to chew off and swallow. Don't buy a wind-up, musical teddy bear; it's not as cuddly, and any small mechanism could come out and get swallowed.

Big wooden beads.

Fat, easy-to-hold beads are fun to hold and drop into containers. An older sibling or you needs to help with the stringing; your baby will be glad to do the unstringing.

Push-and-pull toys.

Babies who can walk like to push and pull lawn mower-type toys with wheels and long handles. With some varieties of these toys children can pretend they are vacuuming or mowing the lawn. Others make satisfying (to children) popping sounds. Still others have wagonlike compartments for transporting things.

Approximate age range: 12 to 18 months

...ONE-AND-A-HALF-YEAR-OLDS

A big, simple dump truck.

Your one-and-a-half-year-old should be able to fill the truck and dump it easily. Don't buy a dump truck that's hard to work or that has a lot of little parts that break off easily.

Barn and farm animals.

Children like animals and enjoy putting small, realistic ones into a barn or box.

Alphabet and number blocks.

Young children like these cubic, hand-size blocks for stacking and dropping into containers.

Should your child be reading the letters and numbers on the blocks?

Your child may learn to name the letters and numbers on the blocks in the same way your child may learn to name a cow or truck. But your child will not be able to read words made from the blocks. Most likely, your child will like the blocks for their size, shape, heft, and construction possibilities. The letters and numbers are less interesting features.

Approximate age range: 12 to 18 months

BODY PARTS

As children learn the names of people and objects in the world about them, they can also learn the names of their own body parts. You can help them do this by naming the parts of their bodies in conversation, games, and songs. One of the favorite skills that babies and parents like to show off to grandparents and baby-sitters is the skill of pointing to parts of the face. For some reason, this activity is immensely enjoyable. Perhaps it is because everyone senses that when babies can point upon request to their own eyes, mouth, and nose they are really somebodies at last.

Approximate age range: 12 to 18 months

SELF-AWARENESS & SELF-ESTEEM

There's a difference between self-awareness and self-esteem. Self-awareness is being aware that you exist as a person separate from other persons. Self-esteem is liking yourself. One is intellectual, the other is emotional. Babies need to develop both, and you can help them. You help them develop self-awareness when you show them what they look like in the mirror, when you talk about their body parts, and when you describe their actions with descriptive words.

You help babies develop self-esteem by showing them that you like them, that you respect them, that they matter to you, and that you will take care of them. No aspect of parenting is more important.

Approximate age range: 12 to 18 months

PILLOW GAME: WHERE'S DADDY?

Disappearance games continue to capture children in this age group because they are still learning the difficult concept of object permanence (see page 93). One of their most delightful experiences is when you play the pillow game called "Where's Daddy?"

To play this game, hold a pillow up in front of your face so that your child can't see you. Then say, "Where's Daddy?" Position yourself close enough so that your baby can reach out and pull down the pillow. When that happens, say, "Here I am!" You can also play this with a magazine, a piece of junk mail, or a napkin. You can add a little extra thrill to the game if you tickle your child for a second or two after you say, "Here I am."

Approximate age range: 12 to 18 months

BABY HIDE-AND-SEEK

Another popular disappearance game is baby hide-and-seek, a simplified variation of the hide-and-seek game older children play. In this game you let your child watch you hide. After you have disappeared behind, say, the couch, you or someone else says, "Where's Daddy? Find Daddy!" This game may seem too easy to you, but for your child, who isn't sure if you have disappeared or not, it is exciting. And if you provide a big hugging welcome upon being discovered, that makes the game even better. Eventually, your child will learn to hide from you and enjoy being discovered. But at first, very young children don't know how to hide. Sometimes they think that they are hidden from view when they close their eyes. They figure if they can't see anything, neither can you! This is a great game for Baby and older siblings to play.

Approximate age range: 12 to 18 months

READING

It's definitely time to start introducing your child to books, if you haven't already done so. Try to make reading to your child a regular activity throughout his or her childhood. There is no better way to interest your child in the world of books and literature.

Babies this age like books with pictures of familiar objects. When you are selecting books for babies, look for those that have clear pictures and an uncluttered design. The books may have either a very simple story or no story at all, just labels for pictures. Most babies are intrigued by the pictures and satisfied if all you do is point to familiar objects and name them. Once babies get used to books, they like to find and point to things, too, especially if you name the things they point to. Eventually, they will name the objects themselves. If the books have a simple yet poetic text, the words may become the first poem you hear your child recite aloud.

Approximate age range: 12 to 18 months

WHERE TO KEEP BABY'S BOOKS

Most children's bookstores and libraries have special sections in which books for very young children are featured. Notice that some of these books are made of sturdy material that children can't rip or eat. You can leave such books in your baby's crib for your baby to read upon waking or on the floor with Baby's toys. Other books have perfect pictures and text for the youngest child but the pages can be torn. Keep these books on a high shelf and bring them out when you have time to read to your child.

Approximate age range: 12 to 18 months

FAMILIAR PEOPLE & STRANGERS

Your child may still act friendly with familiar people and wary with strangers. This is not illogical, so give your hesitant baby an opportunity to get to know newcomers before you expect your baby to warm up to them. Babies who are used to strangers greeting them will have less fear, but you never know when stranger anxiety will manifest itself.

KITCHY KITCHY KOO?

Approximate age range: 12 to 18 months

SHYNESS

At times you may feel embarrassed that your child clings to you in shyness instead of going forward to play with another child or to be hugged by a friendly caregiver. You may notice with regret that other children are less shy and wonder what's wrong with your child. Don't worry too much about shyness. Realize that there may be several reasons for your child's behavior. Some children go through shy stages. Other children are naturally more shy than others and remain so as they mature.

Still other children are shy when they first meet other people. They cling to you for a few minutes, but then, after a while, they decide to let go. Try not to compare your child with others, but accept your child as is. Sometimes you can interest your child in an activity and wait until another child comes over. When the other child joins in and the two children seem happy to be in each other's company, you can withdraw without making a big deal of it.

Approximate age range: 12 to 18 months

PERSONALITY PLUS

By the time children are eighteen months old, they have experienced many complex emotions, ranging from sympathy and worry to jealousy and fury. In other words, your child has a personality now! You'll find it easier to get along with your child if you respect your child as a person who is almost as complex as you are.

Don't expect your child to be even-tempered all the time.

Respond to your child's various moods. When your child's personality is bursting out in a negative way, help your child gain a measure of self-control by identifying the problem and offering a distracting alternative. When your child is bursting with happiness, let it be catching. Your child possesses the wonderful ability to cheer you up. Be receptive.

Approximate age range: 12 to 18 months

THE GOLDEN RULE

A father of three says, "Every time I got confused about how to treat my children (which was often), I tried to remember the Golden Rule: 'Do unto others as you would have them do unto you.' It's a simple guideline to recall in an instant, and it works. If you don't want to be made fun of, don't make fun of your children. If you don't want to be neglected, don't neglect your children. If you don't want to be patronized or overindulged, don't patronize or overindulge your children. Conversely, if what you want is acceptance, fairness, and love—accept, be fair to, and love your kids."

Approximate age range: 12 to 18 months

CONGRATULATIONS, YOUR CHILD'S A TODDLER ...

Your child can now walk, talk, express feelings, and play games. Think back to when your baby was first born—what a difference a year and a half makes! Your child is to be congratulated for working so hard to accomplish so much.

Approximate age range: 18 months

... AND YOU'RE A TODDLER'S FATHER!

And you—in a year and a half you have become an accomplished parent. Your family has developed and grown as an entity. As problems have arisen, you have helped to solve them. You have grown and changed—probably for the better because fatherhood can do that to men. So, take a moment to feel a burst of pride: pride in your child, pride in your family, and pride in yourself as a father, the most important job you'll ever have.

Approximate age range: 18 months

MORE ABOUT THE AUTHOR

Jean Marzollo is the author of many books for children, including *Close Your Eyes, The Teddy Bear Book, Pretend You're a Cat,* and the *I SPY* series. She has also written many books for parents, including *Your Maternity Leave: How to Leave Work, Have a Baby, and Go Back to Work without Getting Lost, Trapped or Sandbagged along the Way.* For twenty years she was the editor of Scholastic's *Let's Find Out* early childhood magazine. She has written about parenting in *Parents Magazine, Working Mother,* and *Family Circle.* She is a graduate of the University of Connecticut and the Harvard Graduate School of Education. She lives with her family in Cold Spring, New York.

MORE ABOUT THE ILLUSTRATOR

Irene Trivas is the author and illustrator of several children's books, including *Annie...Anya: A Month in Moscow* and *Emma's Christmas.* She has illustrated many other children's books, such as *Potluck, The Pain and the Great One, My Mother's House, My Father's House, Who'll Pick Me Up When I Fall?* and *The One in the Middle Is a Green Kangaroo.* Before she began to illustrate picture books, she had a successful career as an animation designer and director. She is a graduate of U.C.L.A. and lives in South Ryegate, Vermont.